SALAD SEASONS

SALAD SEASONS

Vegetable-Forward Dishes All Year

SHEELA PRAKASH

RIZZOLI
NEW YORK

New York · Paris · London · Milan

Contents

Introduction

CONVENTIONAL WISDOM HAS IT THAT THERE IS A SEASON for salads. That season is unquestionably summer. It's the abundance of produce that spills out of farmers markets from June through September, coupled with sultry weather, that signals this truth.

Outside of summer, one salad all too often dominates the dinner table: that omnipresent bowl made from slightly slimy mesclun out of a plastic clamshell. Truly applause-worthy salads are often scarce at home—you might have to drop into that trendy downtown restaurant, where they're doing something chef-y with carrots, to find it.

Here's a little secret, though: salad season can be all seasons—that is, if you know how to build a great one. To start, reach for the best of what is around you. Of course, weighty heirloom tomatoes make for an untouchably good caprese salad, but dead-of-winter cabbage holds as much potential, too. The secret to unlocking this potential is seasoning. We never question seasoning when it comes to other dishes. We diligently shower a boiling pot of pasta water with salt, marinate and glaze our meats, and slather all sorts of condiments between two slices of bread when building sandwiches. Yet, beyond making a basic vinaigrette (or reaching for a bottle of one), we haven't really been taught to season our salads. I am not talking about just salt and pepper—both of which are the absolute foundation (along with great produce, of course) of an extremely tasty salad—but other seemingly simple ingredients that add layers of flavors and textures. If you're wondering just exactly why that chef-y carrot salad was so good, this is your answer: They really, truly seasoned it.

Salad Seasons is a play on words: It's a celebration of the four seasons and a lesson in how smart seasoning can transform your salads. Understand the basics of preparing flavorful salads, lean into the ebb and flow of seasonal produce, and suddenly, it's the salad that's the perpetual star at your table, 365 days a year.

Salad Secrets

A salad isn't meant to be a complicated endeavor. At its most basic, it's a bowl of greens. Arugula dressed with olive oil, lemon juice, flaky salt, and a few grinds of black pepper is a no-fail salad solution in our house. That's just the start, though.

Shake Up What Salad Means

IT'S IMPORTANT TO STATE—RIGHT OFF THE BAT—THAT many of the salads in this book are unconventional. To me, a salad isn't strictly lettuce-centric. It doesn't even need to be served in a bowl or on a plate, either. My definition is a dish that's produce-first, with a dressing that ties all the components together, and layers of flavor and texture that make for fun and interesting forkfuls. It can be a sheet pan situation, where a mix of vegetables and other good things like beans are roasted all together, tossed in something bright and bracing, and brought tableside for everyone to scoop right off the pan, like the Harissa-Roasted Sweet Potato and Chickpea Salad on page 124. Or it can be a platter of grilled vegetables made much more interesting with the help of some slabs of grilled cheese, pickled things, and a sweet-and-savory vinaigrette, such as the Grilled Broccolini and Halloumi Salad on page 94. Of course, classics like the arugula salad on page 18, which I toss in a whole-lemon vinaigrette, apply, too.

Season Well and Often

SALADS NEED TO BE SEASONED WITH SALT AND PEPPER to taste just like anything else you're preparing in the kitchen. That's why instead of calling for a finite amount of salt and pepper in each recipe, I intentionally ask for you to season and taste as you go. It's the quickest way to learn this fundamental rule. Even if you've seasoned the dressing, the lettuce or whatever other vegetables you might be using need a bit of salt and pepper, too. Tasting as you compose your salad and adjusting seasoning right before serving will result in a restaurant-quality salad rather than one that tastes like an afterthought.

While salt and pepper are essential, they're just part of the conversation. Oil (my preference is almost always extra-virgin olive), an array of vinegars and citrus juices, condiments like mustard and miso paste, spices, and fresh herbs lend big flavor. Nuts, seeds, and cheese do, too, as well as provide layered texture.

Think Beyond the Usual Produce

YOU MIGHT NOT THINK PARSNIPS MAKE FOR A DELIGHT-ful salad, but the Honey-Mustard Parsnip and Pancetta Salad on page 188 proves otherwise. Just about any vegetable—raw or cooked—can be the base of an awesome salad. Keep this in mind and suddenly, a salad made with in-season goodies can be on the center of your table even in the depths of winter.

Speaking of produce, I am talking about fruit, too. If you, like me, find fruit salads a disappointment 99.9 percent of the time, know they don't have to be. Apply similar tactics to fruit and you can have a fruit salad for dessert, brunch, or even just a mid afternoon snack that's actually a thrill. Strawberry-Rhubarb Salad with Lavender Honey (page 57), Bourbon-Baked Apples with Cinnamon Toast Croutons (page 154), and Brûléed Citrus Salad (page 205) are just a few.

How This Book Is Organized

EACH SEASONAL CHAPTER IN THIS BOOK IS SPLIT INTO three sections: Side, Star, and Sweet. Side salads are self-explanatory—they're meant to complement your main dish. Star salads, however, aim to be the main event. These salads are heartier, often with things like grains, beans, fish, and meat to round them out. Crusty bread is often all that's needed to complete them. Sweet salads are my playful, offbeat take on fruit salads. They're a nice ending to a meal and some are quite perfect at the brunch or breakfast table, too.

The serving size for each recipe reflects the section it falls into. So a Star salad might serve four, but know that's as a main dish. If you'd rather enjoy it as a side, it will of course stretch to feed a few more mouths.

Seasonings to Keep Stocked

STARTING WITH GOOD-QUALITY, IN-SEASON PRODUCE IS crucial to tasty salads—but so is having smart ingredients at your disposal in your pantry. Here are the items I rely on. Some are basic, others are upgrades.

Oil and Vinegar(s)

EXTRA-VIRGIN OLIVE OIL: Choose a high-quality, well-sourced bottle. There are plenty to splurge on, but I find California Olive Ranch's 100% California extra-virgin olive oil to be an easy-to-find option that transitions from cooking oil to salad dressing oil seamlessly. It's mild, buttery, and extremely reliable. If you're up for keeping two olive oils around, pick a dynamic bottle at your local specialty food shop to finish salads with.

RED WINE VINEGAR: It's a classic for a reason and my most all-purpose vinegar choice.

WHITE WINE VINEGAR: The best choice when clean, bright, and delicate are what you're after.

SHERRY VINEGAR: Heavier-bodied than red and white wine vinegars, but nutty and warming like balsamic. If you've never thought much of sherry vinegar before, seek out true Vinagre de Jerez and you'll quickly be converted. Columela is a trusted brand that's easier to track down than some (I particularly like the thirty-year version, which is surprisingly affordable for a bottle with such age).

BALSAMIC VINEGAR: Make sure the bottle you stock doesn't contain caramel color. You'll be surprised by how many do, and they're not the real deal. While it has a time and place, balsamic on its own can often be too cloying in salads, so I often combine it with red wine vinegar to achieve balance.

APPLE CIDER VINEGAR: If I want a little sweetness without the body of sherry or balsamic vinegar, ACV never fails.

LEMONS: Not a vinegar, but used in the same way. Choose organic, if possible, since both the zest and the juice deliver punch.

Salt, Pepper, and Beyond

KOSHER SALT: Specifically, Diamond Crystal kosher salt, which is the gold standard among recipe developers and chefs. If it isn't already, I hope it becomes yours, too. It's less course and salty than other kosher salt brands, so you have more control when sprinkling it in.

FLAKY SEA SALT: Many of the recipes in this book call for flaky sea salt for serving. Maldon sea salt flakes are irregularly shaped pyramid-like crystals that lend a finishing touch of briny crunch. If there's one pantry upgrade recommended in this book to take advantage of, this is it.

FRESHLY GROUND BLACK PEPPER: The best flavor will always be achieved from grinding the peppercorns directly from a pepper mill.

CHILE FLAKES: I keep a few on hand, including Italian red pepper flakes for classic heat but also Aleppo pepper and Urfa biber chile flakes. The latter two are much milder, which means you can use a heavier hand. Aleppo is fruity and earthy while Urfa biber is smoky, with raisin-like sweetness.

SMOKED PAPRIKA: While any smoked paprika will lend depth of flavor, I try to seek out true Spanish smoked paprika—pimentón de la Vera—which has more character than cheaper grocery store jars. I especially like the hot, or picante, variety, which is a one-two punch of smoke and heat.

SUMAC: This tart, lemon-like spice is the ground dried berries of the sumac bush. It's a wonderful way to add citrusy brightness when your salad doesn't need any more liquid in the form of lemon juice. Speaking of which, za'atar does something a bit similar, albeit different. This Middle Eastern spice blend contains tangy sumac but it also features dried thyme and/or oregano, toasted sesame seeds, and salt. That means it's savory, earthy, and nutty, too. New York Shuk is my favorite brand for both sumac and za'atar.

DIJON MUSTARD: Maille is my ride-or-die brand. I like to keep a regular jar and a jar of whole grain Dijon on hand if I want to add a bit of texture (see Mustardy Carrot Slaw, page 21), but as long as you at least have the former, it helps emulsify dressings and provides creamy tang.

HONEY AND MAPLE SYRUP: When making a salad dressing, oil and vinegar often need to be countered by sweetness. Honey and maple syrup dissolve easily and lend their own distinct flavor.

SHALLOTS: They're milder and sweeter than onions, but provide that same character.

GARLIC: I prefer to grate garlic into dressings using a Microplane, so it disperses evenly. It's also much easier and faster than mincing.

FRESH HERBS: Parsley, cilantro, basil, thyme, dill, rosemary, chives, and more give salads lots of flavor.

Creamy

GREEK YOGURT: Whole-milk plain Greek yogurt is the best choice, but you can also use reduced-fat, if you prefer. It can be swiped into the bottom of bowls before piling salad in or used in dressings.

MAYONNAISE: After living in the South, I now swear by Duke's, which is perfectly rich and smooth and far from gloopy like other jars can be.

TAHINI: Creamy but nutty, too. Soom is my trusted brand.

Crunchy

NUTS AND SEEDS: It doesn't matter if you use almonds, walnuts, pistachios, hazelnuts, pepitas, or sesame seeds. Nuts and seeds are the quickest way to add crunchy texture to a salad. Always toast them beforehand to reveal their true flavor.

SCALLIONS: While thinly sliced scallions lend sharp flavor, too, I especially love sprinkling them on salads for their fresh crunch.

Spring

There's a jolt of excitement that comes with spring's first crops. Bundles of asparagus and stained baskets of strawberries signify we've made it through another long winter and sunnier days are ahead. Verdant green is the color of the season, whether it's in the form of tender young lettuces, juicy snap peas, or soft carrot tops. After months of warming up with heavier fare, it feels good to shed some of the bulk and cook a little lighter.

Arugula Salad with Whole-Lemon Vinaigrette

SERVES 4

¼ cup sliced raw almonds, divided

1 small lemon

1 clove garlic, peeled

1 teaspoon honey

Kosher salt

Freshly ground black pepper

¼ cup extra-virgin olive oil

5 ounces arugula (about 5 packed cups)

NOTES: No food processor? You can still make this vinaigrette by chopping the lemon and almonds by hand. The end result will be a bit rougher in texture but still delicious.

Store leftover vinaigrette right in its jar in the refrigerator for up to a week. I love spooning it on salmon, shrimp, white fish like cod or halibut, or chicken before baking in the oven, where it transforms into a bright and cheerful sauce.

The thought of using an entire lemon—flesh, peel, and all—might sound nothing short of crazy, but it's no-waste brilliance at its very best. Not only are you throwing away half of the citrus fruit when you simply squeeze out its juice and toss the spent halves, you're missing out on big flavor, too. The vibrant peel, bitter pith, and lip-puckering flesh are bold elements that, when combined with buttery almonds, a touch of sweet honey, and a generous glug of olive oil, make for a complex vinaigrette that's unlike anything you've had before. It's the perfect counterpart for just about any type of lettuce, but it's especially lovely with arugula because it balances the greens' peppery bite.

ARRANGE A RACK in the middle of the oven and heat the oven to 350°F.

Spread the almonds out on a baking sheet and toast in the oven, stirring halfway through, until lightly golden, about 5 minutes. Let cool for 5 minutes.

Trim the stem end off the lemon, cut the lemon into quarters, and remove any seeds. Transfer to a food processor fitted with the blade attachment and pulse until roughly chopped, about 15 pulses (see Note). Take a peek to see if you missed any seeds, and if so, remove them with a spoon.

Add half of the almonds, the garlic, honey, a generous pinch of salt, and several grinds of pepper. Pulse until the lemon and almonds are finely chopped, scraping down the sides of the food processor as needed, about 30 pulses more.

Transfer the lemon and almond mixture to an airtight jar or container. Add the olive oil, seal the jar, and shake to combine and emulsify.

Place the arugula in a large salad bowl, drizzle with half the vinaigrette, and toss to combine. Add more vinaigrette, if desired, a spoonful at a time, until the salad is dressed to your liking. Taste and season with additional salt and pepper as needed. Sprinkle with the remaining toasted almonds.

Mustardy Carrot Slaw

SERVES 4 TO 6

2 tablespoons Dijon
mustard

2 tablespoons whole
grain mustard (or use an
additional 2 tablespoons
regular Dijon instead, for
a total of ¼ cup Dijon)

¼ cup extra-virgin
olive oil

3 tablespoons white
wine vinegar

2 teaspoons honey

Kosher salt

Freshly ground black
pepper

2 pounds carrots with
tops

4 scallions (white and
green parts), thinly sliced

Here's a recipe to make as soon as it has warmed up enough to get out and enjoy the first picnic of the season. Pack it up, pick up sandwiches on your way to the park, and find a sunny spot on the grass. You can, of course, enjoy this slaw at home, too. It's tasty right after tossing it together, but know that it gets even better after a few hours of rest, once the dressing has softened the carrots and the flavors marry.

PLACE THE MUSTARD(S), olive oil, vinegar, honey, a generous pinch of salt, and several grinds of pepper in a large bowl. Whisk well to combine and emulsify.

Cut off the carrot tops, then cut off the top feathery leaves and tender stems, discarding the stiff stems at the bottom. Wash and dry the leaves and tender stems well, then finely chop and add them to the bowl. Peel the carrots, grate them in a food processor fitted with the grating attachment or on the large holes of a box grater, then add to the bowl.

Add the scallions and toss well to combine and coat everything in the dressing. Taste and season with additional salt and pepper as needed.

NOTE: This slaw can be made up to a day ahead. Just keep it covered in the refrigerator and let it come to room temperature before serving.

Marinated Fennel Salad with Crispy Fried Capers

SERVES 4

———

5 tablespoons extra-virgin olive oil, divided

1 tablespoon red wine vinegar

Zest of ½ medium lemon

Juice of ½ medium lemon (about 1½ tablespoons)

Kosher salt

Freshly ground black pepper

2 medium or 1 large fennel bulb (about 1½ pounds), trimmed, quartered, and very thinly sliced with a mandoline or knife (reserve ½ cup of the feathery fronds)

3 tablespoons capers (rinsed if salt-packed), drained and patted dry

Fennel is heading out of season in early spring, and even after enjoying it every which way through the winter months, I am still not tired of it. Instead of cooking it, though, I like to keep it raw, to reflect the warmer weather and the desire for something fresh. Here, fennel is shaved thin and tossed in a lemony marinade, then contrasted through the addition of crunchy, salty fried capers. It's not just the bulb that's used, though. I almost always incorporate the feathery fronds, which here lend color and added brightness.

WHISK TOGETHER 2 tablespoons olive oil, the vinegar, lemon zest, lemon juice, a generous pinch of salt, and several grinds of pepper in a large bowl. Add the fennel and toss to coat. Allow to marinate while you fry the capers.

Heat the remaining 3 tablespoons olive oil in a small saucepan over medium-high heat until shimmering. Carefully add the capers to the pot and fry them until crisp on the outside and the outer layer has fanned out a bit, 1 to 2 minutes. Use a slotted spoon or spider to transfer them to a paper towel–lined plate.

Coarsely chop the reserved fronds, add them to the bowl of marinated fennel, and toss to combine. Taste and season with additional salt and pepper as needed, then sprinkle with the fried capers.

Quick-Pickled Radish Salad

SERVES 4

¼ cup apple cider vinegar

2 tablespoons extra-virgin olive oil

1 teaspoon granulated sugar

Kosher salt

Freshly ground black pepper

2 Persian (mini) cucumbers, unpeeled and very thinly sliced with a mandoline or knife

12 medium red or Easter Egg radishes, very thinly sliced with a mandoline or knife

2 medium watermelon radishes, very thinly sliced with a mandoline or knife (cut the sliced rounds in half if very large)

2 tablespoons chopped fresh chives

2 tablespoons chopped fresh dill

It took a CSA (community supported agriculture) membership for me to appreciate radishes. Though our boxes through the spring and summer contained a few more bunches of the vegetable than I'd anticipated when signing up, it forced me to prepare radishes every which way. Quick pickling them became my favorite because it retains and even heightens the vegetables' natural crunch while infusing them with tangy flavor. This is a make-ahead-friendly salad that's simple and bright.

PLACE THE VINEGAR, olive oil, sugar, 1 teaspoon salt, and several grinds of pepper in a large bowl and whisk to combine. Add the cucumbers, radishes, chives, and dill. Toss to combine.

Let rest for at least 30 minutes, tossing occasionally, to allow the flavors to meld. Alternatively, cover and refrigerate overnight. Before serving, taste and season with additional salt and pepper as needed.

Little Gems with Herby Ranch Yogurt

SERVES 4

½ cup whole-milk plain
Greek yogurt

2 tablespoons
mayonnaise

2 tablespoons apple
cider vinegar

2 tablespoons finely
chopped fresh chives

2 tablespoons finely
chopped fresh parsley

1 tablespoon finely
chopped fresh tarragon
leaves

1 clove garlic, grated
or minced

Kosher salt

Freshly ground black
pepper

4 heads Little Gem
lettuce (about 10 ounces
total), halved lengthwise

½ small lemon

Flaky sea salt, for serving

Chive blossoms, for
serving (optional)

When Little Gem lettuce pops up at my local farmers market, the miniature heads are gone in a matter of an hour or two. They're a fan favorite, and it's easy to understand why: The heirloom lettuce is a small variety of romaine that's incredibly sweet and tender—almost like butter lettuce but with the juicy crunch of romaine. Creamy homemade ranch dressing, bolstered with thick and tangy Greek yogurt, is a wonderful complement. If you can't find Little Gem heads, mini baby heads of romaine can be used, or try half the amount of small romaine hearts.

STIR TOGETHER THE yogurt, mayonnaise, apple cider vinegar, chives, parsley, tarragon, garlic, a generous pinch of kosher salt, and several grinds of pepper in a small bowl. Taste and season with additional salt and pepper as needed.

Spread half of the ranch yogurt evenly on a serving platter, then arrange the lettuce, cut sides up, on top. Squeeze the juice from the lemon half over the top, drizzle with the remaining yogurt, and sprinkle with flaky sea salt. If using chive blossoms, gently tear them apart and scatter the petals over the salad.

Wilted Dandelion Green Salad

SERVES 4 TO 6

2 bunches dandelion greens (about 1 pound)

2 tablespoons extra-virgin olive oil

1 clove garlic, thinly sliced

2 tablespoons apple cider vinegar

2 teaspoons honey

Kosher salt

Freshly ground black pepper

¼ teaspoon Aleppo pepper or Urfa biber chile flakes, plus more for serving

Flaky sea salt, for serving

Dandelion greens are probably shooting up from undesirable locations in your backyard right now. You'll also find them being sold in big bunches at the farmers market or your local grocery store. The weed is, in fact, edible, and absolutely delicious at that—so long as you know how to prepare it. Skip those from your yard and parks, though, unless you're absolutely sure they haven't been sprayed with chemicals or the dog hasn't gotten to them. The deep-green, thin-stemmed leaves are bitter, so they need to be tamed with sweetness and some vinegar. Both are utilized here, in a warm honey-garlic vinaigrette punctuated by your choice of mild chile flakes. Aleppo pepper is sweet and fruity, while Urfa biber is pleasantly smoky. The vinaigrette softens the leaves and makes them approachable but still very much their peppery selves.

TRIM THE TOUGH lower stems off the dandelion greens and discard. Tear the leaves on their tender stems into bite-sized pieces and place in a large bowl. Using your hands, massage the leaves until they're softened and feel less stiff, 1 to 2 minutes.

Heat the olive oil in a small saucepan over low heat until shimmering. Add the garlic and cook, stirring occasionally, until very fragrant, 1 to 2 minutes. Add the vinegar, honey, a generous pinch of kosher salt, a few grinds of pepper, and the Aleppo pepper or Urfa biber chile flakes and whisk until combined and warmed through, less than 1 minute.

Immediately drizzle the warm vinaigrette over the greens and toss to coat and wilt. Taste and season with additional kosher salt and pepper as needed. Garnish with a couple of generous pinches of chile flakes and a big pinch of flaky sea salt.

Scorched Sugar Snap and Burrata Salad

SERVES 4

3 tablespoons extra-virgin olive oil, divided, plus more for serving

½ medium red onion, thinly sliced

Kosher salt

Freshly ground black pepper

1 pound sugar snap peas, tough strings removed

Juice of 1 lemon (3 tablespoons)

¼ cup loosely packed chopped fresh mint leaves

1 teaspoon ground sumac, plus more for serving

1 (8-ounce) ball or 2 (4-ounce) balls burrata cheese

Flaky sea salt, for serving

I am not quite sure why, but sugar snap peas delight me. Yes, you might be rolling your eyes right now (I know my husband, Joe, surely would be), but bear with me. Sugar snaps are a fleeting spring vegetable that really signal the season, as they're hard to find outside of it, and even if you manage it, they're just never as sweet. Their juicy crunch is a welcome respite after bulkier winter vegetables. I let sugar snaps lead in this salad by simply searing them in a hot skillet and tossing them in a lemony vinaigrette. They're paired with a creamy ball of burrata to round out the meal.

HEAT 2 TABLESPOONS of the olive oil in a large cast-iron or other heavy-bottomed skillet over medium-high heat until shimmering. Add the red onion, season with a generous pinch of kosher salt and a few grinds of pepper, and cook, stirring occasionally, until softened and lightly browned in spots, 3 to 4 minutes. Transfer to a large bowl.

Add the snap peas to the skillet in a single layer and cook, undisturbed, until charred in spots on the bottom, 2 to 4 minutes. Season with a generous pinch of kosher salt and several grinds of pepper and stir. Continue to cook, stirring occasionally, until crisp-tender and lightly browned in spots all over, about 2 minutes more. Transfer to the bowl of red onion.

Add the remaining 1 tablespoon olive oil, the lemon juice, mint, and sumac to the bowl, then toss to combine. Taste and season with additional kosher salt and pepper, as needed.

Place the burrata in the center of a serving platter and spoon the snap pea mixture around the burrata. Drizzle with a little more olive oil and sprinkle with a little more sumac and a few pinches of flaky sea salt.

Roasted Halibut Niçoise Salad

SERVES 4

6 tablespoons extra-virgin olive oil, divided

2 tablespoons red wine vinegar

Juice of ½ medium lemon (about 1½ tablespoons)

1 clove garlic, grated or minced

2 teaspoons Dijon mustard

Kosher salt

Freshly ground black pepper

1 (1½-pound) skinless halibut fillet

8 ounces fingerling potatoes, halved lengthwise

8 ounces thick asparagus, woody ends trimmed, cut into 2-inch pieces on the bias

8 medium radishes, halved

1 large head butter lettuce (about 12 ounces), such as Boston or Bibb, leaves torn

½ cup Castelvetrano olives, pitted and roughly chopped

8 fresh basil leaves

Flaky sea salt, for serving

Halibut, given its price, is a special occasion fish in my opinion. This riff on classic French salade niçoise, however, is absolutely an occasion. It brings together some of the heavy hitters of spring produce: asparagus, radishes, fingerling potatoes, and tender green lettuce. The meaty, mild-tasting fish doesn't overpower these seasonal favorites. Instead, each delicate ingredient holds its own in the bowl. Buttery green Castelvetrano olives and a tangy Dijon vinaigrette make it complete. Yes, this salad is definitely a reason to break out warm weather's first bottle of rosé.

ARRANGE A RACK in the middle of the oven and heat the oven to 425°F.

Meanwhile, whisk together 4 tablespoons of the olive oil, the vinegar, lemon juice, garlic, Dijon, ½ teaspoon kosher salt, and several grinds of pepper in a small bowl until combined and emulsified. Transfer 3 tablespoons of the vinaigrette to a baking dish just large enough to hold the halibut. Season the halibut all over with kosher salt and pepper, then place in the baking dish, turning it over gently a few times to evenly coat in the vinaigrette. Refrigerate, uncovered, while you begin to roast the potatoes.

Toss the potatoes with 1 tablespoon olive oil, ½ teaspoon kosher salt, and several grinds of pepper in a large bowl. Transfer the potatoes to a rimmed baking sheet and arrange so they are cut side down. Roast without flipping until the potatoes are lightly browned on the bottom and they easily release from the pan with a flat spatula, about 15 minutes.

Meanwhile, place the asparagus and radishes in the now-empty bowl and toss with the remaining 1 tablespoon olive oil, ½ teaspoon kosher salt, and several grinds of pepper.

Toss the potatoes and add the asparagus and radishes to the baking sheet. Toss to combine, then push the vegetables to one side to create space for the halibut. Transfer the halibut to the empty space, drizzle with any remaining marinade in the dish, and return the baking sheet to the oven. Roast until the vegetables are tender and the fish is opaque and flakes easily with a fork, 10 to 20 minutes, depending on the thickness of your fillet.

Meanwhile, whisk the reserved vinaigrette once or twice more to ensure it's emulsified. Toss the lettuce with half of the reserved vinaigrette in the now-empty bowl. Taste and season with additional kosher salt and pepper as needed. Divide the dressed lettuce among 4 plates or shallow bowls.

Once the fish and vegetables are cooked, top the dressed lettuce with the roasted vegetables. Use a fork to break the fish into large irregular pieces and arrange over each serving. Sprinkle with the olives and drizzle everything with the remaining vinaigrette. Tear basil leaves over the top and finish with a few grinds of pepper and a pinch or two of flaky sea salt.

Spring Carrots with
Burnt Saffron Butter and Labneh

SERVES 4

2 pounds carrots

4 tablespoons unsalted butter

¼ teaspoon saffron threads

Juice of ½ medium lemon (about 1½ tablespoons)

Kosher salt

Freshly ground black pepper

¼ cup raw hazelnuts

1½ cups labneh

Chopped fresh parsley, for serving

Flaky sea salt, for serving

While carrots are available 365 days a year, they especially shine in the spring, at their peak season. This recipe brings them to the center of your plate. Carrots are roasted in a brown butter sauce enhanced with floral saffron and piled atop creamy, soft, and tangy labneh, a Middle Eastern yogurt cheese. A handful of chopped fresh parsley and sweet toasted hazelnuts tie it all together. Definitely serve this platter with crusty bread or pillowy pita so you can swipe it clean.

Labneh is made by straining whole-milk plain yogurt until it's even thicker than Greek yogurt and closer to the consistency of cream cheese. While it was once hard to find outside of Middle Eastern markets, you'll now find it at some Whole Foods and other well-stocked grocery stores. Otherwise, you can make it quite easily yourself by simply straining Greek yogurt (see page 36).

ARRANGE 2 RACKS to divide the oven into thirds and heat the oven to 425°F.

Peel and trim the carrots. I love leaving the carrots whole, since fresh spring carrots tend to be smaller than the year-round carrots you find in bags at the grocery store, but if the carrots you're using are quite long and you prefer, cut them in half crosswise. If they are more than 1 inch in diameter, cut them in half lengthwise. Place on a rimmed baking sheet; set aside.

Melt the butter in a small saucepan over medium heat. Add the saffron and continue cooking, swirling the pan occasionally, until the butter has a nutty aroma and is a toasty-brown color, about 3 minutes. Remove from the heat, carefully add the lemon juice (it will spatter) and a pinch of kosher salt, and stir to combine, scraping up any browned bits at the bottom of the pan with a wooden spoon.

Drizzle half of the saffron butter sauce over the carrots. Sprinkle with ½ teaspoon kosher salt and several grinds of pepper and toss to coat again. Spread the carrots into a single layer. Roast on the bottom rack for 15 minutes.

Meanwhile, spread the hazelnuts out on a rimmed baking sheet and toast on the top rack, stirring halfway through, until fragrant and golden brown, 5 to 7 minutes. Let the nuts cool for 5 minutes.

Flip the carrots, then roast them until the carrots are tender and the edges are charred and crispy, 15 to 20 minutes more.

Wrap the toasted hazelnuts in a clean kitchen towel and rub vigorously to remove as much of the skins as possible (don't worry about any skin that doesn't easily come off). Transfer the nuts to a cutting board and coarsely chop.

Spread the labneh out in a large, even layer on a serving platter with the back of a spoon. Place the roasted carrots on top of the labneh. Drizzle the remaining half of the brown butter sauce over the carrots, then sprinkle with the hazelnuts, parsley, and a generous pinch of flaky sea salt.

A Little More About Labneh

Can't find labneh? To make your own, combine 2 cups whole-milk plain Greek yogurt and ½ teaspoon kosher salt in a medium bowl. Line a fine-mesh strainer with a couple of layers of cheesecloth and set it over a bowl. Place the yogurt mixture in the strainer, cover the top with plastic wrap, and let drain in the fridge for 24 hours.

Labneh is traditionally enjoyed as a dip or spread, or even rolled into balls and marinated in olive oil and spices and served as part of a mezze or breakfast platter. For me, nothing beats serving it simply in a bowl, topped generously with olive oil and za'atar, and paired with crudités, pita chips, or torn flatbread. It's also wonderful dolloped on fresh fruit and drizzled with honey in place of your usual morning yogurt.

Tortellini Salad with Garlic Scape Pesto

SERVES 4

Kosher salt

10 garlic scapes, roughly chopped (about ½ cup)

¼ cup roasted and lightly salted shelled pistachios

⅓ cup extra-virgin olive oil

½ ounce Pecorino Romano cheese, freshly grated (¼ packed cup)

Juice of 1 medium lemon (about 3 tablespoons)

1 (9- or 10-ounce) package fresh or frozen cheese tortellini

8 ounces thick asparagus, woody ends trimmed, cut into 2-inch pieces on the bias

1 small head radicchio (about 6 ounces), halved lengthwise, cored, and thinly sliced

2 ounces arugula (about 2 packed cups)

1 cup loosely packed fresh basil leaves

Freshly ground black pepper

Freshly shaved Pecorino Romano cheese, for serving

Stop by the farmers market in late May or so, and you'll find bundles of thin, curly green stalks that look a bit like they have a mind of their own. They're garlic scapes—the stalks that grow from the bulbs of garlic plants that are harvested before they flower so that the plants can then go on to use their energy to grow the bulbs below the soil. Garlic scapes are wildly garlicky but also sweet and pleasantly grassy. They can be sautéed or grilled, but they're especially nice blended into pesto, where salty Pecorino stands up to the scapes' commanding flavor. This is a vegetable-packed pasta salad that's bursting with seasonal flair.

BRING A LARGE pot of salted water to a boil over high heat. Meanwhile, make the garlic scape pesto.

Place the garlic scapes and pistachios in the bowl of a food processor fitted with the blade attachment and pulse a few times until roughly chopped.

Add the olive oil, cheese, and lemon juice. Process, stopping to scrape down the sides of the bowl as needed, until the mixture comes together into a rough paste. Taste and season with salt as needed. Set aside.

Add the tortellini to the boiling water and cook according to the package instructions for al dente. One minute before the tortellini are finished cooking, add the asparagus directly to the pasta water with the tortellini. Drain the tortellini and asparagus together in a colander and run briefly under cool water to cool down. Drain well again.

Return the tortellini and asparagus to the pot, off the heat. Add the pesto and toss to coat. Add the radicchio and arugula and tear the basil leaves into the pot. Toss gently to combine. Taste and season with salt and pepper as needed. Transfer the tortellini salad to a serving bowl or individual shallow bowls and garnish with shaved Pecorino.

Warm Spinach-Artichoke Salad with Quinoa Crunchies

SERVES 4

½ cup quinoa

¾ cup water

Kosher salt

2 (12-ounce) jars marinated quartered artichoke hearts, drained

2 tablespoons extra-virgin olive oil, plus more for serving

Freshly ground black pepper

5 ounces baby spinach (about 5 packed cups)

Juice of ½ medium lemon (about 1½ tablespoons)

3 ounces feta cheese, crumbled (about ¾ cup)

2 scallions (white and green parts), thinly sliced

While it's hard to beat the flavor and texture of fresh spring artichokes, they're a bit tedious to work with and they're not always readily available. That means I often rely on jarred artichokes when I want my fix. It's a shortcut with an added benefit: When you drain a jar of marinated artichoke hearts and roast them, they brown and crisp at the edges beautifully. Toss them with tender baby spinach leaves and top the mix with crunchy toasted quinoa, scallions, and feta crumbles for a light yet warming bowl.

ARRANGE 2 RACKS to divide the oven into thirds and heat the oven to 450°F.

Place the quinoa in a fine-mesh strainer and rinse well. Transfer the quinoa to a small saucepan, add the water and ¼ teaspoon salt, and bring to a boil over high heat. Reduce the heat to low, cover, and simmer until the quinoa is tender and all the liquid is absorbed, about 15 minutes. Uncover and fluff with a fork. Taste and season with additional salt as needed. Transfer the quinoa to a rimmed baking sheet, spread into an even layer, and refrigerate to cool while you roast the artichokes.

Meanwhile, place the artichokes on a rimmed baking sheet, toss with the olive oil, ¼ teaspoon salt, and several grinds of pepper, and spread into a single layer. Roast on the bottom rack, tossing halfway through, until browned, 18 to 20 minutes. Remove from the oven and immediately scatter the baby spinach over the roasted artichokes to very lightly wilt while you toast the quinoa. Switch the oven to broil on high.

Use your fingers to break up any large clumps of quinoa, ensuring it's spread into a single layer. Transfer the baking sheet of quinoa to the top rack and broil, tossing frequently, until the quinoa is browned and crispy, 5 to 7 minutes.

Gently toss the vegetables with the lemon juice, a generous pinch of salt, and several grinds of pepper on the baking sheet. Taste and season with additional salt and pepper as needed. Divide among 4 individual plates or shallow bowls. Sprinkle with quinoa crunchies, feta, and scallions and drizzle with olive oil.

Spicy Smashed Cucumbers with Chickpea Scallion Pancakes

SERVES 4

1 cup chickpea flour

1 cup water

3 tablespoons plus 2 teaspoons extra-virgin olive oil, divided

Kosher salt

2 pounds English or Persian (mini) cucumbers (about 2 large English or 12 Persian)

4 scallions (white and green parts), thinly sliced

1½ tablespoons rice vinegar

1 tablespoon Asian chili garlic sauce, such as Huy Fong

1 tablespoon low-sodium soy sauce or tamari

1 teaspoon grated peeled fresh ginger

1 teaspoon toasted sesame oil

1 small clove garlic, grated or minced

2 medium avocados, pitted, peeled, and diced

1½ tablespoons raw sesame seeds

I'll take a cool, crisp cucumber salad any which way, but lately, I can't stop leaning on this surprising technique that truly makes for the best cucumber salad of all. Smashing your cucumbers is not only a fun stress reliever, it's common practice in Chinese cooking, and results in all sorts of nooks and crannies for dressing to latch on to. The slightly broken-down cucumber flesh is also able to soak up more of it. Grab a zip-top bag and something heavy, such as a rolling pin or skillet, to crush the vegetable, then toss the pieces with salt to help them release some of their water, so you're left with cucumbers that are concentrated in flavor and ready to grab whatever dressing you throw at them.

Here, the dressing is a spicy, ginger- and sesame-infused one that's quick to pull together. The heat comes from Asian chili garlic sauce, Sriracha's less popular sibling. Like Sriracha, Huy Fong is the most widely available brand of Asian chili garlic sauce and you'll find it right next to Sriracha at the grocery store in a small plastic jar. It has a permanent spot in my refrigerator—I love its bright spice that's countered with a punch of garlic.

While this salad is light and refreshing on its own, it becomes a meal when paired with scallion pancake wedges made from protein-rich (and naturally gluten-free) chickpea flour. It's hardly authentic but I think you'll agree it's pretty darn tasty.

WHISK TOGETHER THE chickpea flour, water, 1 tablespoon olive oil, and ½ teaspoon salt in a medium bowl until smooth. Cover and let the mixture rest at room temperature to give the flour time to absorb the water, 30 minutes.

Leave the cucumbers unpeeled, then trim the ends off, cut each crosswise into 4 pieces, and place in a large zip-top bag. Seal the bag, then firmly but gently smash the cucumbers with a rolling pin or heavy pot or skillet a few times until the pieces are about ½ inch thick.

Tear into roughly 1-inch pieces, if using English cucumbers; if using Persian cucumbers, they should already be roughly that size, so no need to tear. Place the smashed cucumbers in a colander set over a large bowl. Sprinkle with ½ teaspoon salt and toss to combine. Let stand to release some of their water while you bake the scallion pancake.

Arrange a rack in the top third of the oven (6 to 8 inches from the broiling element) and heat the oven to 450°F. You want to get the entire oven nice and hot before broiling the pancake, so it cooks evenly.

Place a 10-inch cast-iron skillet in the oven and turn on the broiler. Let it sit under the broiler for 5 minutes. Do your best to skim off most of the foam that has formed on the surface of the chickpea flour batter and discard. Stir the scallions into the batter.

Carefully remove the hot skillet from the oven. Add 2 tablespoons olive oil and carefully swirl to coat the bottom of the pan. Pour the batter into the skillet and return it to the oven. Broil until the edges of the flatbread are set, the center is firm, and the top is lightly browned in spots, 6 to 10 minutes. Meanwhile, dress the cucumber salad.

Remove the colander from the bowl. Discard any accumulated liquid in the bowl. To this bowl, add the rice wine vinegar, Asian chili garlic sauce, soy sauce, remaining 2 teaspoons olive oil, the ginger, toasted sesame oil, and garlic. Whisk well to combine. Add the cucumbers and avocado to the bowl and toss gently to coat. Taste and season with additional salt as needed.

Remove the scallion pancake from the oven. Let cool while you toast the sesame seeds.

Place the sesame seeds in a small skillet and toast over medium heat stirring frequently, until lightly golden brown and fragrant, about 5 minutes. Transfer to a small bowl.

Carefully slide a flat spatula under the scallion pancake and transfer it to a cutting board. Slice into 8 wedges. With a slotted spoon, divide the cucumber salad among 4 shallow bowls or plates and place 2 wedges of the scallion pancake on the side of each bowl. Sprinkle with the toasted sesame seeds.

Charred Leeks and Asparagus with Jammy Eggs

SERVES 4

4 large eggs

4 large or 6 medium leeks

1 pound thick asparagus, woody ends trimmed

5 tablespoons extra-virgin olive oil, divided

Kosher salt

Freshly ground black pepper

2 tablespoons sherry vinegar

½ teaspoon smoked paprika (pimentón de la Vera), preferably hot, or picante

⅓ cup panko bread crumbs

1 clove garlic, grated or minced

Flaky sea salt, for serving

This salad is very loosely inspired by asparagus mimosa, a classic French dish of asparagus spears drizzled with vinaigrette and topped with grated hard-boiled egg. Here, the asparagus is broiled rather than blanched, and paired with sweet leeks. Both are dressed with a smoky sherry vinaigrette, completed with creamy soft-boiled eggs, and because I can't help but add crunch, a smattering of garlicky toasted bread crumbs.

LET THE EGGS rest on the counter to take their chill off from the fridge—this will help prevent them from cracking when boiled. Bring a medium saucepan of water to a boil. Arrange a rack in the top third of the oven (6 to 8 inches from the broiling element) and preheat the broiler to high.

Trim the root ends of the leeks and the dark green tops. Cut each leek in half lengthwise and remove any tough outer layers. Rinse the leek halves well under cold water to remove any dirt in between the layers, then pat dry.

Place the leeks, cut side up, on a rimmed baking sheet and add the asparagus. Drizzle the vegetables with 2 tablespoons olive oil and season with ½ teaspoon kosher salt and several grinds of pepper. Gently toss to coat, then return the leeks cut side up.

Carefully lower the eggs into the boiling water with a slotted spoon. Boil, uncovered, for 7 minutes for soft-boiled eggs with jammy, but not runny, yolks. Fill a medium bowl with ice and water.

Whisk together 2 tablespoons olive oil, the vinegar, smoked paprika, a generous pinch of kosher salt, and a few grinds of pepper in a small bowl until combined and emulsified. Taste and season with additional salt and pepper as needed.

Transfer the baking sheet of leeks and asparagus to the oven and broil until tender and charred, 5 to 10 minutes.

recipe continues . . .

Once the eggs are cooked, transfer them to the ice bath with a slotted spoon and chill until cold, about 5 minutes.

Meanwhile, heat the remaining 1 tablespoon olive oil in a small skillet over medium heat until shimmering. Add the bread crumbs, garlic, and a pinch of kosher salt. Toast, stirring frequently, until golden brown, 3 to 5 minutes. Transfer to a small bowl.

Remove the eggs from the ice bath, then peel and halve lengthwise. Transfer the leeks and asparagus to a serving platter and arrange the halved eggs among them. Spoon the vinaigrette over the top, scatter with the toasted bread crumbs, and sprinkle with a pinch of flaky sea salt.

Spring Pea and Orzo Salad with Bacon Gremolata

SERVES 4

6 slices bacon (about 6 ounces, not thick-cut)

Kosher salt

8 ounces dried orzo pasta (about 1⅔ cups)

10 ounces fresh or frozen shelled peas (about 2 cups)

½ cup loosely packed finely chopped fresh parsley

1 clove garlic, grated or minced

Finely grated zest of 1 medium lemon

Juice of 1 medium lemon (about 3 tablespoons)

Freshly ground black pepper

Gremolata is an Italian condiment of finely chopped fresh parsley, minced garlic, and lemon zest that is most traditionally used to provide brightness to luxuriously rich osso buco, a classic Milanese dish of braised veal shanks. It packs a punch of freshness to just about anything, as is the case here. This is definitely not an authentic gremolata, as I've added chopped crispy bacon to it since the orzo salad it's brightening is not all that inherently heavy, and a little salty decadence won't hurt one bit.

ARRANGE A RACK in the bottom third of the oven and heat the oven to 400°F. Line a rimmed baking sheet with parchment paper so that there is overhang on all 4 sides. (This prevents the bacon drippings from seeping over the edges of the parchment paper, making for easier cleanup later.)

Lay the bacon on the baking sheet in a single layer. Bake on the bottom rack until deep golden brown and crispy, 12 to 15 minutes. Remove from the oven, then transfer the bacon to a paper towel–lined plate to drain and cool. Reserve the bacon grease on the baking sheet to use in the salad.

Meanwhile, bring a medium pot of salted water to a boil. Add the orzo to the water and cook until 1 minute before al dente, about 8 minutes or according to the package instructions. One minute before the orzo finishes cooking, add the peas to the pasta water with the orzo and blanch until bright green and crisp-tender. Drain the orzo and peas together in a colander and run briefly under cool water to cool down. Drain well again.

Once the bacon is cool, transfer it to a cutting board and coarsely chop. Combine the chopped bacon with the parsley, garlic, and lemon zest in a medium bowl.

Transfer the orzo and peas to a large serving bowl and toss with 2 tablespoons of the reserved bacon grease, the lemon juice, a generous pinch of salt, and several grinds of pepper. Stir in half of the gremolata, then taste and season with additional salt and pepper as needed. Top with the remaining gremolata.

Roast Chicken Salad with Herbes de Provence, Escarole, and Brie

SERVES 4

7 tablespoons olive oil, divided

3 tablespoons herbes de Provence

1 (3½- to 4-pound) whole chicken, at room temperature

Kosher salt

Freshly ground black pepper

1 medium lemon

1½ tablespoons red wine vinegar

2 teaspoons Dijon mustard

1 clove garlic, grated or minced

1 teaspoon honey

1 medium head escarole (about 1 pound)

6 ounces Brie cheese, torn into chunks

This salad is equal parts elegant and comforting. Serving the herb-infused carved chicken over a bed of dressed escarole isn't just pretty, it helps to gently wilt the leaves and ensures they soak up the meat's juices. It's the torn pieces of buttery Brie that really make this dinner a showstopper, though. They soften with the heat of the chicken, too, and become perfectly gooey, creamy mouthfuls to latch on to with your fork.

ARRANGE A RACK in the middle of the oven and heat the oven to 450°F.

Combine 3 tablespoons of the olive oil and the herbes de Provence in a small bowl. Pat the chicken dry with a paper towel. Using your fingers, gently loosen and pull away the skin from the breasts, legs, and back. Stuff the herb oil under the skin, little by little, spreading it against the meat all over the breasts, legs, and back.

Generously season the chicken on all sides, inside and out, with salt and pepper. Place the chicken, breast side up, in a large baking dish, roasting pan, or cast-iron skillet. Halve the lemon crosswise and squeeze the juice from one half over the top of the chicken. Reserve the remaining lemon half and stuff the squeezed lemon half into the chicken's cavity.

Transfer the baking dish to the oven and immediately lower the oven temperature to 400°F. Roast until an instant-read thermometer inserted into the thickest part of the chicken thigh reads 170°F, the wings and legs feel loose when you wiggle them gently, and the juices run clear, 1 to 1½ hours. Transfer the chicken to a cutting board and let rest for 10 minutes while you assemble the salad.

Squeeze the juice from the remaining lemon half (about 1½ tablespoons) into a large bowl. Add the remaining 4 tablespoons olive oil, the vinegar, Dijon, garlic, honey, a generous pinch of salt, and several grinds of pepper. Whisk well to combine and emulsify.

   If there are any very tough outer dark green or brown
leaves on the head of escarole, remove and discard them. Tear
the remaining leaves into bite-sized pieces, add to the bowl of
vinaigrette, and toss to coat. Taste and season with additional
salt and pepper as needed. Spread the dressed escarole out on a
serving platter.

   Carve the chicken and place the carved pieces on top of the
dressed escarole on the platter. Tear the Brie—rind and all—into
bite-sized chunks and scatter over the escarole and chicken.

White Bean–Avocado Salad with Radish Salsa

SERVES 4

1 medium bunch radishes with tops (about 10)

½ cup loosely packed chopped fresh cilantro

2 scallions (white and green parts), thinly sliced

1 small serrano pepper, finely chopped

3 medium limes, divided

2 tablespoons extra-virgin olive oil, divided

Kosher salt

Freshly ground black pepper

2 (15-ounce) cans white beans, drained and rinsed

1 clove garlic, grated or minced

2 medium avocados, pitted, peeled, and diced

Creamy white beans and avocado chunks, while delicious, need some crunchy contrast to be successful together in a salad. That's why, though both are important players here, it's the radish salsa that's the true star. It's bright, crisp, and perfectly peppery. When piled on top of the bean salad, you have a quick and colorful bowl.

TRIM THE TOPS from the radishes and reserve. Finely dice the radishes and place them in a medium bowl. Add the cilantro, scallions, and serrano pepper. Squeeze the juice of 2 limes (about ¼ cup) into the bowl. Add 1 tablespoon olive oil, season with a generous pinch of salt and a few grinds of pepper, and toss to combine. Taste and season with additional salt and pepper as needed. Set aside.

Remove and discard any yellowed radish leaves and tear the remaining leaves into bite-sized pieces into a large bowl. Squeeze the juice of the remaining lime (about 2 tablespoons) into the bowl. Add the white beans, garlic, remaining 1 tablespoon olive oil, a few generous pinches of salt, and several grinds of pepper. Toss to combine. Add the avocados and toss gently to combine. Taste and season with additional salt and pepper as needed. Divide the white bean salad among 4 shallow bowls and top with radish salsa.

Herbed New Potato and Salmon Salad

SERVES 4

¼ cup white wine vinegar

¼ teaspoon granulated sugar

Kosher salt

Freshly ground black pepper

1 medium shallot, halved lengthwise and thinly sliced

2 pounds new potatoes, or baby red or Yukon Gold potatoes (no larger than 1½ inches in diameter)

¼ cup extra-virgin olive oil

2 tablespoons fresh thyme leaves

2 (4-ounce) packages hot-smoked salmon

Nothing against the smoked salmon squished between a bagel and cream cheese, but it's the other smoked salmon that really has my heart. I'm talking about hot-smoked salmon, which is cured and smoked with heat the same way meat can be. The other, more familiar, smoked salmon is cold-smoked, which means it's cured and smoked at a low temperature so that it doesn't cook and is served thinly sliced. Hot-smoked salmon is firm and totally cooked through—it actually looks a whole lot like a regular piece of cooked salmon. What I love about it is that, well, I don't have to cook it, and yet I still get the texture of cooked salmon with the added bonus of deep smoky flavor. It's also readily available by the fish counter at your grocery store. Here, it's flaked into a simple potato salad that makes for a satisfying spring main, especially if you wash it down with a crisp, cold glass of white wine.

WHISK TOGETHER THE vinegar, sugar, ½ teaspoon salt, and several grinds of pepper in a large bowl. Add the shallot and toss to coat. Set aside to pickle while you cook the potatoes.

Place the potatoes and 1 tablespoon salt in a large saucepan. Cover by 1 inch with cool water, then bring to a boil over high heat. Reduce the heat to medium and simmer until the potatoes are easily pierced with a knife, 10 to 15 minutes. Drain in a colander and rinse under cold water until cool enough to handle but still warm.

Add the olive oil and thyme to the bowl of shallots and whisk well to combine and emulsify.

Halve the potatoes and transfer to the bowl of vinaigrette. Gently toss to coat the potatoes. Flake the salmon into bite-sized pieces with a fork, add to the bowl, and toss lightly to combine. Set aside for 10 minutes to allow the flavors to meld. Taste and season with additional salt and pepper as needed. Serve warm or at room temperature.

Strawberry-Rhubarb Salad with Lavender Honey

SERVES 4

⅓ cup mild-flavored honey, such as orange blossom or clover

1 teaspoon dried food-grade lavender buds

1 tablespoon fresh lemon juice

Kosher salt

2 stalks rhubarb, thinly sliced on the bias

⅓ cup raw almonds

1 pound strawberries, hulled and halved (or quartered, if large)

1 teaspoon fresh lemon thyme or thyme leaves

NOTE: You'll have a little extra lavender-infused honey. Drizzle it on yogurt, biscuits, or scones, stir it into tea or coffee, or use it to sweeten lemonade and cocktails.

I have a vivid childhood recollection of playing in a friend's yard and snacking on rhubarb stalks fresh from the plant. Of course, it's probably ingrained in my memory because of how wildly sour raw rhubarb is. That's why it's almost always cooked with sugar or another sweetener to counteract its tartness. However, it's possible for it to be unexpectedly enchanting when raw. This unique fruit salad showcases how raw rhubarb can sweeten up when tossed with honey, which macerates it and draws out some of its natural sugars. It's still quite tangy, though, so strawberries—rhubarb's lifelong partner—provide balance. The fun is in the juicy crunch raw rhubarb retains, which for me, at least, tastes of a spring garden.

PLACE THE HONEY and dried lavender buds in a small saucepan over low heat and warm gently until the mixture is fragrant, about 10 minutes. Remove from the heat, cover, and let steep for 10 minutes.

Strain the honey through a fine-mesh strainer into an airtight container. Transfer 2 tablespoons of the lavender-infused honey to a large bowl. Cover and refrigerate the remaining honey for up to 1 month.

Add the lemon juice and a pinch of salt to the bowl and whisk. Add the rhubarb and toss to coat. Set aside for 30 minutes to allow the rhubarb to soften and release some of its juices.

Meanwhile, arrange a rack in the middle of the oven and heat the oven to 350°F.

Spread the almonds out on a baking sheet and toast in the oven, stirring halfway through, until fragrant and golden brown, 8 to 10 minutes. Let cool for 5 minutes, then roughly chop.

Add the strawberries, almonds, and thyme to the bowl. Gently toss to combine.

Roasted Apricots with Cardamom Cream and Pistachios

SERVES 4

10 green cardamom pods

1 cup heavy cream, divided

2 pounds fresh apricots (about 20)

¼ cup honey, plus more for serving

2 teaspoons fresh lemon juice

Kosher salt

¼ cup shelled pistachios (either raw and unsalted or roasted and lightly salted)

The season for perfectly ripe, sweet apricots is a fleeting one. Since I live on the East Coast, where the rosy stone fruit isn't quite as abundant, I am often left with tart, less-than-perfect apricots that I still want so desperately to enjoy while they're available. That's why I frequently find myself roasting them, which helps draw out the fruits' jammy juices. Here, they're folded into an aromatic cardamom-infused whipped cream for a fool-like dessert— a traditional English treat—that's simple and light.

ARRANGE A RACK in the middle of the oven and heat the oven to 350°F.

Crush the cardamom pods with the bottom of a small saucepan. Place the crushed pods and any cardamom seeds that popped out in the saucepan. Pour ½ cup heavy cream into the saucepan and reserve the remaining ½ cup heavy cream in the refrigerator to keep it cold.

Bring the cream and cardamom mixture to a simmer over medium heat. Reduce the heat to low and simmer gently to warm and infuse the cream, 2 to 3 minutes. Remove from the heat and continue to let steep, covered, while you roast the apricots.

Quarter the apricots by halving and pitting them, then cutting each apricot half into two wedges. Place the apricot wedges in a 9 x 13-inch baking dish. Drizzle with the honey and lemon juice, and sprinkle with a pinch of salt. Toss and spread into an even layer. Roast, tossing gently halfway through, until some juices have released and the fruit is quite tender and softened, 20 to 30 minutes. Let cool until just warm to the touch while you toast the pistachios, if needed.

If using raw pistachios, spread the pistachios out on a baking sheet. Transfer to the oven and toast, stirring halfway through, until fragrant and golden, 6 to 8 minutes. Let cool for a few minutes, then coarsely chop.

Stir the cardamom-infused cream (it likely will have thick-ened and formed a skin), then pour it through a fine-mesh strainer into the bowl of a stand mixer fitted with the whisk attachment or into a large bowl, if using a hand mixer. Press the cream and cardamom pods firmly with the back of a spoon to release all of the infused cream through the strainer. Add the reserved ½ cup cold heavy cream. Beat on medium-high speed until medium peaks form, 2 to 4 minutes.

Add about two-thirds of the apricots to the whipped cream and fold gently with a rubber spatula to just combine. Divide the mixture among individual serving bowls and top with the remaining roasted apricots. Garnish with the pistachios and a generous drizzle of honey.

Balsamic–Black Pepper Cherries

SERVES 4

¼ cup balsamic vinegar

1 tablespoon brown sugar

Kosher salt

1 pound fresh sweet cherries (about 3 cups), pitted and halved

¼ teaspoon coarsely ground black pepper

Mascarpone cheese, for serving

Sugar-rich, in-season cherries don't need much tinkering. Aside from eating them simply out of hand, I like to toss the stone fruit with syrupy balsamic vinegar and coarsely ground black pepper. You may have tried this trick with strawberries, but it works just as nicely, if not better, with cherries. Both the vinegar and pepper draw out the inky sweetness and intensify the fruit's juices. Serve bowls topped with a dollop of creamy mascarpone and nothing else.

COMBINE THE BALSAMIC vinegar, brown sugar, and a pinch of salt in a small saucepan and bring to a boil over medium-high heat. Reduce the heat to medium and simmer, stirring occasionally, until the sugar has dissolved and the mixture has reduced by half and is syrupy, about 5 minutes. Remove from the heat and let cool for 5 minutes.

Toss the cherries with the reduced balsamic vinegar and pepper in a large bowl. Let sit for 10 minutes. Divide among individual glasses or bowls and top with a dollop of mascarpone.

Summer

This abundant season hardly needs an introduction. Truthfully, it's a bit of a show-off. Head to the farmers market midsummer and you're greeted by a rainbow of colors, all vying for your attention. Between curiously shaped heirloom tomatoes, taut eggplant and zucchini, and fuzzy peaches, you're sure to head home with a heavy load. Tossing together a salad is almost a no-brainer this time of year. It's easy to eat well when so much great produce is at your disposal. With the grill, oven (if you're willing to turn it on), stovetop, and often just a cutting board and sharp knife, you can have even more fun than you might expect.

Cherry Tomato Salad with Knife Pesto Vinaigrette

SERVES 4

———

1 small clove garlic, smashed and peeled

1 cup packed fresh basil leaves

2 tablespoons roasted and lightly salted shelled pistachios

3 tablespoons extra-virgin olive oil

2 tablespoons white wine vinegar

2 tablespoons freshly grated Parmesan cheese

Freshly ground black pepper

2 pints cherry or grape tomatoes (about 4 cups), preferably multicolored, halved

Kosher salt

While I am the first to say the food processor is what I reach for most when making pesto, true pesto is actually made with a mortar and pestle or, better yet, a mezzaluna. This curved, crescent moon–shaped knife has a handle on each end and rocks back and forth over whatever you're chopping. I don't own a mezzaluna, but a sharp chef's knife works similarly to achieve a wonderfully rustic, texture-rich pesto that isn't over blended. Knife pesto, as I like to call it, is also a great option when you're making just a small batch. I happen to think all the chopping is pretty cathartic, too.

ROUGHLY CHOP THE garlic clove. Pile the basil leaves and pistachios on top of the chopped garlic and finely chop altogether. Transfer the mixture to a large bowl.

Stir in the olive oil, vinegar, Parmesan, and a few grinds of pepper. Add the tomatoes and toss to coat. Taste and season with salt and additional pepper as needed.

Israeli Corn Salad

SERVES 4 TO 6

1 medium shallot, diced into ¼-inch pieces

2 ears sweet corn, shucked and kernels removed (about 1¼ cups)

½ large English cucumber, diced into ¼-inch pieces

2 medium plum or Roma tomatoes, diced into ¼-inch pieces

Juice of 1 medium lemon (about 3 tablespoons)

2 tablespoons extra-virgin olive oil

1 tablespoon za'atar, plus more for serving

Kosher salt

Freshly ground black pepper

2 tablespoons chopped fresh mint leaves

¼ cup loosely packed chopped fresh parsley

The corn in this riff on Israeli salad isn't cooked, and that's not a typo. Peak-season summer corn is so juicy and sweet, it's unexpectedly delicious raw. The key is to seek out the freshest-possible ears and use them as soon as you can—ideally the same day. That's because the kernels' natural sugars begin to turn to starch as soon as the ears are picked. While the same buying rule applies when you're cooking corn, it's especially important here, since starchy corn equates to mealy, flavorless corn even more so when raw.

RINSE THE DICED shallot in a fine-mesh strainer with cool water to make it less potent. Drain well and place it in a large bowl.

Add the corn, cucumber, tomatoes, lemon juice, olive oil, za'atar, a few generous pinches of salt, and several grinds of pepper to the bowl and toss well to combine. Taste and season with additional salt and pepper as needed. Stir in the mint and parsley. Garnish with more za'atar before serving.

Smoky Grilled Eggplant with Feta and Mint

SERVES 4

½ cup extra-virgin olive oil, divided

¼ cup sherry vinegar

1½ teaspoons smoked paprika (pimentón de la Vera), preferably hot, or picante

1 clove garlic, grated or minced

Kosher salt

Freshly ground black pepper

2 small eggplants (about 1½ pounds total), sliced in ½-inch-thick rounds

Handful fresh mint leaves

4 ounces feta cheese, crumbled (about 1 cup)

The soft flesh of an eggplant is a total sponge. The secret to great-tasting eggplant is to utilize this feature. Here, thick rounds of eggplant are grilled plainly just to tenderize them and get them charred. Only after this are they tossed with a smoky vinaigrette. Marinating the vegetable post-grill means it absorbs and locks in the savory combination of olive oil, sherry vinegar, garlic, and smoked paprika. Finish things off with a healthy dose of crumbled feta and torn fresh mint and you have a perfect summer side.

HEAT AN OUTDOOR grill for medium-high direct heat.

Meanwhile, whisk together ¼ cup olive oil, the vinegar, smoked paprika, garlic, a generous pinch of salt, and several grinds of pepper in a large, shallow dish, such as a 9 x 13-inch baking dish. Taste and season with additional salt and pepper as needed.

Lay the eggplant slices on a baking sheet. Brush the remaining ¼ cup olive oil on both sides of the slices and season all over with salt and pepper.

When the grill is hot, grill the eggplant, covered, until grill marks appear, 3 to 5 minutes. Flip and continue to grill until grill marks appear on the other side and the slices are very tender, about 2 to 3 minutes more.

Transfer the eggplant to the dish with the dressing. Flip gently to coat, then marinate, flipping once or twice more, for 15 minutes.

Arrange the eggplant slices in an overlapping pattern on a serving platter, then drizzle with any remaining dressing in the baking dish, if desired. Tear the mint leaves into small pieces, if large; otherwise, keep them whole. Sprinkle the feta and mint over the eggplant.

Simple Summer Greens

SERVES 4

1 oil-packed anchovy fillet

1 small clove garlic, smashed and peeled

2 tablespoons extra-virgin olive oil

Juice of 1 medium lemon (about 3 tablespoons)

1 teaspoon Dijon mustard

Freshly ground black pepper

5 ounces tender lettuce, mixed greens, or arugula (about 5 packed cups)

Kosher salt

Flaky sea salt, for serving

Of all the various vinaigrettes and dressings in this book, this is probably the one my husband, Joe, and I make the most. It's Caesar-ish, thanks to garlic and anchovy, while lots of lemon juice makes it bright and bracing. Dijon gives it a bit of creaminess without actual cream or cheese, and it comes together in a mortar and pestle, which gives it a rustic, extra-homemade quality. We're anchovy enthusiasts, and if I had a soapbox to stand on to profess my zeal for the tiny fish, I would. I know they're not for everyone, but if you like the savory bite of Caesar dressing, you'll absolutely love this.

MASH THE ANCHOVY and garlic clove into a rough paste in a mortar and pestle. Add the olive oil, lemon juice, Dijon, and several grinds of pepper. Stir vigorously until combined and emulsified.

Tear the lettuce into bite-sized pieces, if needed, and place in a large bowl. Drizzle with the vinaigrette and toss to coat. Taste and season with kosher salt and additional pepper as needed, then sprinkle with a generous pinch of flaky sea salt.

Creamy Herb-Packed Cucumber Salad

SERVES 4

1 pound English or Persian (mini) cucumbers (about 2 medium or 1 large English or 6 Persian), or a combination of the two, unpeeled and very thinly sliced with a mandoline or knife

Kosher salt

½ small red onion, very thinly sliced

Juice of 1 medium lime (about 2 tablespoons)

¼ teaspoon granulated sugar

Freshly ground black pepper

¼ cup sour cream

1 tablespoon extra-virgin olive oil

½ cup loosely packed chopped fresh herbs, such as dill, parsley, cilantro, mint, and/or basil

A simple cucumber salad is one of my favorite summer side dishes because of how cooling and versatile it is. This is very much a classic one, made lightly creamy with sour cream and full of fresh herbs. Dill is most expected, but I like to use a mix of whatever herbs are looking good in our garden.

PLACE THE CUCUMBERS in a colander set over a large bowl. Sprinkle with ¼ teaspoon salt and toss to combine. Let stand for 30 minutes at room temperature, so the cucumbers release some of their water.

Meanwhile, place the onion, lime juice, sugar, a generous pinch of salt, and several grinds of pepper in a large bowl. Toss to coat the onions and set aside to pickle while the cucumbers stand, tossing once or twice.

Gently pat the cucumbers dry with a paper towel. Add the cucumbers, sour cream, and olive oil to the bowl with the onion and toss to combine. Taste and season with additional salt and pepper as needed. Stir in the herbs.

Grilled Romaine with Tomato Vinaigrette

SERVES 4

---

1 medium beefsteak
or heirloom tomato
(about ½ pound)

1 small clove garlic, gently
smashed and peeled

1 tablespoon balsamic
vinegar

1 tablespoon plus
2 teaspoons extra-virgin
olive oil, divided

½ teaspoon Dijon
mustard

1 tablespoon chopped
fresh basil leaves

Kosher salt

Freshly ground black
pepper

2 medium romaine
lettuce hearts (about
1 pound total), halved
lengthwise through
the core

Lettuce probably isn't the first vegetable you might consider tossing on the grill, but I think it should be. Grilling a sturdy head of lettuce like romaine transforms it, giving it charred, frilly edges while still keeping the bulk of the matter crisp and juicy. When halved lengthwise, the heads reveal layers of nooks and crannies for dressing to nestle in. I like opting for a vinaigrette with a bit of texture. Here, fresh tomatoes are grated on a box grater over a bowl to catch all their juices and soft, pulpy flesh. A little olive oil, balsamic, garlic, Dijon, and fresh basil turn it into a vibrant tomato vinaigrette.

HEAT AN OUTDOOR grill for medium-high direct heat.

Meanwhile, set a box grater over a medium bowl and use the side with the large holes for grating the tomato into the bowl. Discard the flattened skin and stem left behind. Grate the garlic into the bowl with the small holes of the grater. Add the vinegar, 2 teaspoons olive oil, the Dijon, basil, a generous pinch of salt, and a few grinds of pepper. Whisk until combined and emulsified. Taste and season with additional salt and pepper as needed.

When the grill is hot, brush the cut sides of the lettuce with the remaining 1 tablespoon olive oil and season all over with salt and pepper. Grill cut side down, uncovered, until the edges are browned and grill marks appear, 1 to 2 minutes. Flip and grill the other side, about 1 minute more.

Transfer the romaine, cut side up, to a serving platter and spoon the tomato vinaigrette over it.

Farro Tabbouleh with Whipped Tahini

SERVES 4

Kosher salt

1 cup pearled or semi-pearled farro, rinsed and drained

½ cup well-stirred tahini

Zest of 1 medium lemon

Juice of 2 medium lemons (about 6 tablespoons), divided

¼ cup cold water

¼ cup whole-milk plain Greek yogurt

¼ teaspoon ground cumin

3 tablespoons extra-virgin olive oil, plus more for serving

Freshly ground black pepper

1 large tomato, seeded and diced

1 cup loosely packed chopped fresh parsley

¼ cup loosely packed chopped fresh mint leaves

½ large English cucumber, unpeeled and diced

2 scallions (white and green parts), thinly sliced

Flaky sea salt, for serving

Tabbouleh—the Middle Eastern herb salad packed with fresh parsley and mint—is traditionally made with bulgur wheat. I love making it with farro, however, because the chewy, larger whole grains don't get lost in the salad. It results in something that feels so much heartier and meal-worthy, especially when it's piled onto a bed of tahini sauce that's been whipped with Greek yogurt until it's ethereally creamy. On its own, the tabbouleh will taste quite lemony and tart, but forkfuls find their balance from the nutty whipped tahini at the bottom of the bowl.

BRING A LARGE pot of salted water to a boil over high heat. Add the farro to the boiling water and cook according to the package directions until al dente (it should be tender but have a slight chew in the center), 10 to 30 minutes, depending on type. When the farro is ready, drain well and return it to the pot off the heat. Cover and set aside to steam for 10 minutes. Meanwhile, make the whipped tahini.

Place the tahini, lemon zest, and 1½ tablespoons lemon juice (from ½ lemon) in the bowl of a food processor fitted with the blade attachment. Process until the tahini has lightened in texture, about 5 minutes. Scrape down the sides and bottom of the bowl. With the motor running, slowly stream in the cold water. Scrape down the sides and bottom of the bowl, add the yogurt, cumin, and ½ teaspoon kosher salt, and process until whipped and very fluffy, about 1 minute. Scrape down the sides and bottom of the bowl once more, then process again to make sure everything is well blended and smooth, about 30 seconds more.

Whisk together the olive oil, remaining lemon juice (about 4½ tablespoons), a generous pinch of kosher salt, and several grinds pepper in a large bowl until combined and emulsified. Add the farro and toss to coat. Set aside for 5 minutes to cool and allow the grains to absorb some of the dressing.

Add the tomato, parsley, mint, cucumber, and scallions to the farro and toss to combine. Taste and season with additional kosher salt and pepper as needed.

Divide the whipped tahini among 4 shallow bowls or plates and spread it out in a large, even circle with the back of a spoon. Top with the farro tabbouleh, then finish each bowl with a good drizzle of olive oil and a pinch or two of flaky sea salt.

Torn and Marinated Zucchini with Blistered Corn

SERVES 4

2 pounds zucchini (about 4 medium)

6 tablespoons extra-virgin olive oil, divided

Kosher salt

Freshly ground black pepper

1 tablespoon red wine vinegar

2 cloves garlic, thinly sliced

1 tablespoon fresh thyme leaves

¼ teaspoon red pepper flakes, plus more for serving

3 ears sweet corn, shucked and kernels removed

Handful fresh basil leaves

Flaky sea salt, for serving

I am constantly trying to find new ways to enjoy zucchini, because truthfully, the usual approaches are all pretty lackluster to me. So when I discovered torn zucchini, a technique I learned from chef and cookbook author Samin Nosrat, I was quickly starstruck. It's a reverse cooking method that's extremely fun to execute. I don't even bother cutting the zucchini to start. Instead, you'll simply broil the whole squashes until they're just knife-tender. This lazy approach prevents them from overcooking. Once cool enough to handle, you'll quite literally tear the tender zucchini into rough pieces—the craggy edges allow for flavor from a dressing or marinade to soak right in.

ARRANGE A RACK in the top third of the oven (6 to 8 inches from the broiling element) and preheat the broiler to high.

Place the zucchini on a rimmed baking sheet (no need to trim, peel, or cut them just yet). Drizzle with 1 tablespoon olive oil and rub to coat. Season all over with kosher salt and black pepper. Broil until tender (a knife inserted in the center goes in easily) and charred in spots all over, turning the zucchini a few times to evenly brown, 10 to 15 minutes. Transfer the zucchini to a cutting board, turn off the broiler, and let the zucchini cool for a few minutes while you prepare the marinade.

Whisk together 3 tablespoons olive oil, the vinegar, garlic, thyme, red pepper flakes, ½ teaspoon kosher salt, and a few grinds of black pepper in a large bowl.

Trim the stem ends off the zucchini and carefully halve the zucchini lengthwise (they'll release steam). Continue to let cool while you prepare the corn.

Heat 1 tablespoon olive oil in a large cast-iron or other heavy-bottomed skillet over medium-high heat until shimmering. Add half of the corn kernels in a single layer and cook, undisturbed, until charred underneath, 1 to 2 minutes. Toss, season with a big pinch of kosher salt and several grinds of black pepper, and continue to cook, tossing occasionally, until charred all over, 2 to 3 minutes more. Transfer to a large serving platter, spread out in a single layer, and repeat with the remaining 1 tablespoon olive oil and the corn.

Once the zucchini are cool enough to handle, tear them into uneven, roughly 2-inch pieces and add to the bowl of marinade. Toss to coat, then let marinate, tossing a few more times, for 30 minutes.

Transfer the zucchini to the serving platter of corn with a slotted spoon, nestling the pieces among the corn. Tear the basil leaves over the top. Drizzle with a spoonful or two of the marinade remaining in the bowl and finish with a few pinches of flaky sea salt and red pepper flakes.

Balsamic Steak with Caramelized Peppers and Gorgonzola

SERVES 4

———

⅓ cup plus 4 tablespoons extra-virgin olive oil, divided

¼ cup plus 1 tablespoon balsamic vinegar, divided

4 cloves garlic, grated or minced

1 tablespoon Dijon mustard

1 tablespoon fresh thyme leaves

Kosher salt

Freshly ground black pepper

1½ pounds flank steak

3 large bell peppers (about 10 ounces each, preferably a mix of red, orange, and yellow), seeded and thinly sliced

4 ounces arugula (about 4 packed cups)

3 ounces Gorgonzola cheese, crumbled (about ¾ cup)

2 scallions (white and green parts), thinly sliced

While roasted red bell peppers are ubiquitous, I happen to think caramelized peppers—in a mix of colors—are even more intriguing. When the vegetable is thinly sliced and tossed into a fiery skillet, its natural sugars are released, resulting in tender, wilted peppers with deep, concentrated sweetness and splotches of char. Truthfully, I'd happily eat them straight out of the skillet and call it a meal, but then this showstopping salad wouldn't be brought to life, which would be a real shame. Here, arugula and garlicky, balsamic-rich steak join the party, while funky blue cheese and a showering of scallions tie it all together. It's a summer dinner that's pretty hard to compete with.

COMBINE ⅓ CUP olive oil, ¼ cup balsamic vinegar, the garlic, Dijon, thyme, 1 teaspoon salt, and several grinds pepper in a shallow dish large enough to hold the steak. (Alternatively, combine the ingredients in a large zip-top bag.)

Add the flank steak and coat well in the marinade, using your hands to rub it into the meat. Cover (or seal, if using a zip-top bag) and refrigerate for at least 1 hour and up to 24 hours.

When ready to cook, heat 2 tablespoons olive oil in a large skillet over medium heat until shimmering. Add the bell peppers, season with a generous pinch of salt and several grinds of pepper, and sauté, reducing the heat if they start to burn, until soft and caramelized, 18 to 20 minutes. Transfer to a large bowl and reserve.

To cook the steak on the grill: Heat half of an outdoor grill for high direct heat. Heat the other half for medium direct heat. As the grill preheats, take the steak out of the refrigerator to take some of the chill off.

Remove the steak from the marinade, gently shaking off any excess marinade, and place over high heat. Cover and grill until grill marks appear, about 3 minutes, then flip, cover, and grill until grill marks appear on the second side, about 3 minutes more. Flip again and move the steak to medium heat.

Cover and continue grilling until nicely browned and firm, 3 to 5 minutes more. An instant-read thermometer inserted into the thickest part of the steak should read 115° to 120°F for rare steak, 120° to 125°F for medium-rare steak, and 130° to 135°F for medium steak.

To cook the steak in the oven: Arrange a rack in the top third of the oven. Place a large cast-iron skillet or a roasting pan large enough to hold the steak on the rack and heat the oven to 450°F. As the oven preheats, take the steak out of the refrigerator to take some of the chill off.

Remove the steak from the marinade, gently shaking off any excess marinade, and carefully place in the hot skillet. Return the skillet to the oven. Cook for 5 minutes, flip, then continue to cook until nicely browned and firm, 2 to 4 minutes more. An instant-read thermometer inserted into the thickest part of the steak should read 115° to 120°F for rare steak, 120° to 125°F for medium-rare steak, and 130° to 135°F for medium steak.

Transfer the steak to a cutting board and let rest for 10 minutes. Meanwhile, drizzle the remaining 2 tablespoons olive oil and 1 tablespoon balsamic vinegar into the bowl of caramelized peppers. Add the arugula, a pinch of salt, and a few grinds of pepper, and toss to coat. Taste and season with additional salt and pepper as needed.

Spread the mixture out on a serving platter. Slice the steak thinly against the grain and arrange it on top, in the center of the platter. Sprinkle the salad with the Gorgonzola and scallions.

Grilled BLT Chopped Wedge

SERVES 4

¼ cup mayonnaise

¼ cup sour cream

2 tablespoons extra-virgin olive oil, plus more for grilling the lettuce

2 tablespoons finely chopped fresh chives

Juice of ½ lemon (about 1½ tablespoons)

1 teaspoon Dijon mustard

Kosher salt

Freshly ground black pepper

8 slices bacon (about 8 ounces)

1 medium head iceberg lettuce (about 1½ pounds), outer leaves removed, head quartered through the core

1 pint cherry or grape tomatoes (about 2 cups), halved

1 medium avocado, pitted, peeled, and diced

I wait all year for a peak-summer BLT. When tomatoes are at their sweetest and juiciest, it just doesn't really get much better. This mash-up of the sandwich and a classic wedge salad allows for you not to have to wait until mid-August for the best tomatoes, since cherry tomatoes come into their own much earlier in the season and are also quite serviceable off-season. (The Burst Cherry Tomato and Garlic Bread Caprese on page 185 is proof.) Here, chopped grilled lettuce, crispy bacon, creamy chive dressing, and, for good measure, diced avocado, tie the BLT vibes all together.

HEAT HALF OF an outdoor grill for medium-high direct heat. Place a large cast-iron skillet on the direct-heat side of the grill to preheat.

Meanwhile, stir together the mayonnaise, sour cream, olive oil, chives, lemon juice, Dijon, a generous pinch of salt, and several grinds of pepper in a small bowl.

When the grill is hot, place as many bacon slices as will fit in a single layer in the cast-iron skillet. Grill, covered, until deep golden brown underneath, 5 to 8 minutes. Flip and continue to grill, covered, until crispy, 2 to 4 minutes more. Use tongs to transfer the bacon to a paper towel–lined plate. Repeat with the remaining bacon, then carefully transfer the empty skillet to the cool half of the grill to cool down while you grill the lettuce.

Brush the cut sides of the iceberg wedges with olive oil and season all over with salt and pepper. Grill, uncovered, until the edges are browned and grill marks appear, 1 to 2 minutes. Turn to brown the other cut side, 1 to 2 minutes more.

Coarsely chop the iceberg wedges, place in a large bowl, and toss with half of the dressing. Chop the bacon into bite-sized pieces and add to the bowl, along with the cherry tomatoes. Toss together. Taste and season with additional salt and pepper as needed. Divide among 4 shallow bowls or plates and top with the avocado. Drizzle with the remaining dressing, if desired, and garnish with several more grinds of pepper.

Tangy Three-Bean Salad
with Olives and Herbs

SERVES 4 TO 6

Kosher salt

8 ounces green beans, trimmed and cut into 1-inch pieces on the bias

¼ cup apple cider vinegar

3 tablespoons extra-virgin olive oil

1 tablespoon Dijon mustard

1 teaspoon honey

Freshly ground black pepper

2 (15-ounce) cans chickpeas, drained and rinsed

1 (15-ounce) can white beans, drained and rinsed

1 cup pitted Kalamata olives, halved

½ cup loosely packed chopped fresh cilantro

½ cup loosely packed chopped fresh parsley

2 tablespoons chopped fresh mint leaves

Three-bean salad is good old retro American summer fare but truthfully, I could really do without the kidney beans that typically make up part of the equation. They just never seem to soak up the dressing quite as well as the others. So, here's my own interpretation, with white beans taking the place of red beans; they're creamier, and their thinner skin absorbs so much more flavor. A honey-Dijon dressing lends sweetness, which is countered by a generous handful of salty Kalamata olives and lots of chopped fresh herbs. While three-bean salad is typically served as a side dish, it's absolutely packed with enough protein to hold its own as a main.

BRING A MEDIUM saucepan of salted water to a boil over high heat. Meanwhile, fill a medium bowl with ice and water.

Add the green beans to the boiling water and cook until they are vibrant green and crisp-tender, about 2 minutes. Transfer the green beans to the ice bath with a slotted spoon and chill while you make the dressing.

Whisk together the vinegar, olive oil, Dijon, honey, a couple generous pinches of salt, and several grinds of pepper in a large bowl until combined and emulsified.

Remove the green beans from the ice bath, pat dry, and add them to the bowl of dressing. Add the chickpeas, white beans, and olives. Toss well to combine. Taste and season with additional salt and pepper as needed, then stir in the cilantro, parsley, and mint.

Summer Slaw with Hot Honey Shrimp

SERVES 4 TO 6

½ small (1- to 1½-pound) or ¼ medium (2- to 3-pound) head green cabbage, thinly sliced (about 4 cups)

½ small (1- to 1½-pound) or ¼ medium (2- to 3-pound) head red cabbage, thinly sliced (about 4 cups)

Kosher salt

3 tablespoons plus 1 teaspoon hot honey, such as Red Clay or Mike's, divided

3 tablespoons extra-virgin olive oil, divided

2 cloves garlic, grated or minced, divided

1 pound uncooked medium peeled and deveined shrimp

Freshly ground black pepper

¼ cup loosely packed finely chopped fresh cilantro, plus a handful of cilantro leaves for serving

Juice of 2 medium limes (about ¼ cup)

3 medium carrots, peeled and grated (about 1½ cups)

2 scallions (white and green parts), thinly sliced

1 cup coarsely crushed tortilla chips

While hot honey is indeed trendy, it's a trend I endorse. I love how it brings sweet heat to everything from grilled chicken and pizza to cocktails and vanilla ice cream. It's simple to make (see how in the sidebar opposite), but there are some great small brands out there if you want to go the store-bought route. Here, I use it as a glaze for quick-cooking roasted shrimp, which is piled on a colorful, citrusy coleslaw to turn it into dinner. A scattering of salty crushed tortilla chips is the icing on the cake.

ARRANGE A RACK in the middle of the oven and heat the oven to 400°F.

Place the shredded cabbages in a colander set over a bowl and sprinkle with 1 tablespoon salt. Massage and squeeze the cabbage with your hands to help it release its liquid and begin wilting. Set aside to drain for about 15 minutes while you roast the shrimp and make the dressing.

Whisk together 2 tablespoons hot honey, 1 tablespoon olive oil, and half of the grated or minced garlic (1 clove) in a small bowl.

Place the shrimp on a rimmed baking sheet, season with ½ teaspoon salt and several grinds of pepper, and drizzle with the hot honey mixture. Toss to coat and spread out in a single layer. Roast, tossing halfway through, until the shrimp are just opaque, 5 to 8 minutes.

Meanwhile, stir together the cilantro, lime juice, remaining 2 tablespoons olive oil, 1 teaspoon of the hot honey, the remaining garlic, a few big pinches of salt, and several grinds of pepper in a large bowl.

Using your hands, squeeze the cabbage of its excess liquid one handful at a time and add it to the bowl of dressing. Add the carrots and scallions and toss to combine. Taste and season with additional salt and pepper as needed.

Top the slaw with the shrimp and drizzle with the remaining 1 tablespoon hot honey. Garnish with the crushed tortilla chips and cilantro leaves.

How to Make Your Own Hot Honey

If you'd like to make your own hot honey, heat ½ cup mild-flavored honey, such as clover or orange blossom, with 1 tablespoon red pepper flakes in a small saucepan over medium-low heat. Stir the mixture occasionally until it's just warmed through, about 5 minutes. Remove from the heat, cover, and let steep for at least 10 minutes. Taste, and if you'd like it spicier, let it continue to steep until it's to your preferred heat level. Strain the warm honey through a fine-mesh strainer, pressing down on it with the back of a spoon, into an airtight jar or storage container. Stir in a splash of apple cider vinegar and store at room temperature for up to 1 month.

Crispy Tofu and Sesame Noodle Salad

SERVES 4 TO 6

1 (14- to 16-ounce) block super-firm (high-protein) tofu

2 tablespoons cornstarch

¾ teaspoon kosher salt

2 tablespoons vegetable oil, such as grapeseed or canola

4 tablespoons low-sodium soy sauce or tamari

3 tablespoons Chinese rice vinegar

3 tablespoons toasted sesame oil

3 tablespoons well-stirred tahini

1 tablespoon smooth peanut butter

1 tablespoon light or dark brown sugar

1 tablespoon Asian chili garlic sauce, such as Huy Fong, plus more for serving

2 tablespoons grated peeled fresh ginger

2 cloves garlic, grated

1 pound dried rice noodles

2 Persian (mini) cucumbers, unpeeled and thinly sliced

¼ cup roasted salted peanuts, roughly chopped

¼ cup loosely packed chopped fresh cilantro

2 scallions (white and green parts), thinly sliced

I've always hated the process of pressing out tofu with paper towels and the weight of a heavy pan—even firm tofu was still too soft and damp for my taste after doing so. Then I discovered super-firm tofu. This type of tofu isn't water-packed and is indeed seriously firm. It can be sliced right out of the package and holds together when cooked. Tossing cubes in a bit of cornstarch ensures they brown and crisp perfectly. I hope you, like me, never look back. Wildwood and Nasoya are two common brands.

This cold noodle salad is creamy and crunchy, light yet hearty all at once, which is all you could ask for from a dinner in the middle of a sticky summer.

PAT THE TOFU dry with a paper towel. Cut the tofu into 1-inch cubes and place in a medium bowl. Sprinkle with the cornstarch and salt and gently toss to coat.

Heat the vegetable oil in a large cast-iron or other heavy-bottomed skillet over medium-high heat until shimmering. Add the tofu cubes in a single layer and cook, undisturbed, until the bottoms release from the pan easily and are deep golden brown, 3 to 5 minutes. Flip the tofu and continue to pan-fry until the second side is well browned and crisp, 3 to 5 minutes more. (You can continue to brown the four remaining sides, but deeply browning just the top and bottom of the cubes makes them plenty crispy.) Transfer the browned tofu to a wire rack.

Bring a large pot of salted water to a boil. Meanwhile, whisk together the soy sauce, rice vinegar, sesame oil, tahini, peanut butter, brown sugar, chili garlic sauce, ginger, and garlic in a large bowl. Set aside.

Add the rice noodles to the boiling water and cook according to the package directions. Drain the noodles and rinse under cold running water. Drain well.

Add the noodles and tofu to the bowl of dressing and toss to evenly coat. Divide the mixture among individual serving bowls. Top with the cucumbers, peanuts, cilantro, and scallions. Serve with more chili garlic sauce, if desired.

Grilled Broccolini and Halloumi Salad

SERVES 4

1½ pounds Broccolini (about 3 bunches)

7 tablespoons extra-virgin olive oil, divided

Kosher salt

Freshly ground black pepper

1 pound Halloumi cheese, sliced into ½-inch-thick slabs

Juice of 1 medium orange (about ¼ cup)

1 tablespoon white wine vinegar

2 tablespoons chopped fresh oregano leaves

¼ teaspoon red pepper flakes

20 Peppadew peppers, torn (about ¾ cup)

If you're unfamiliar with Halloumi, it's a salty, springy-textured cheese from Cyprus that holds magical powers because it doesn't melt when heated. Instead, it warms, just gently softens, and takes on color from the oven, stovetop, or grill. It's a fun way to add protein and big flavor to a meat-less meal, like this grilled salad. Thanks to thinner stalks, Broccolini cooks faster and more evenly than broccoli on the grill. Once their frilly florets are charred and their stalks are knife-tender, they're tossed in a savory orange-oregano vinaigrette, then piled with slabs of grilled Halloumi and hot and tangy Peppadew peppers.

HEAT AN OUTDOOR grill for medium-high direct heat.

Trim about ½ inch off the bottom of the Broccolini stems. If any of the stems are very thick, cut the Broccolini in half length-wise through the stem and florets. Place the Broccolini on half of a rimmed baking sheet. Drizzle with 2 tablespoons olive oil, ½ teaspoon salt, and several grinds of black pepper and toss to coat. Place the Halloumi slabs on the other half of the pan, drizzle with 1 tablespoon olive oil, and rub to evenly coat both sides.

Whisk together the remaining 4 tablespoons olive oil, the orange juice, vinegar, oregano, red pepper flakes, and a generous pinch of salt in a small bowl.

When the grill is hot, add the Broccolini and grill, covered, turning with tongs halfway through, until tender and charred in spots, 5 to 8 minutes. Return the Broccolini to one half of the baking sheet.

Place the Halloumi on the grill and grill, uncovered, until grill marks appear, 2 to 3 minutes. Flip and continue to grill until grill marks appear on the other side. Return the Halloumi to the other half of the baking sheet.

Drizzle the Broccolini with the vinaigrette and use tongs to toss to coat. Taste and season with additional salt and pepper as needed. Arrange the Broccolini on a serving platter, leaving space in between each stalk. Arrange the Halloumi among the Broccolini. Scatter the Peppadew peppers over the top, drizzle with any vinaigrette that remains on the baking sheet, and serve.

Escalivada Panzanella

SERVES 4

1 large eggplant
(about 1½ pounds)

2 large red bell peppers
(about 1¼ pounds total)

2 large yellow bell peppers
(about 1¼ pounds total)

1 small yellow onion

¼ cup plus 4 tablespoons
extra-virgin olive oil,
divided

Kosher salt

Freshly ground black
pepper

¾ of a good sourdough or
country-style bread loaf,
sliced or torn into roughly
1-inch cubes (about
6 cups)

¼ cup sherry vinegar

1 clove garlic, grated or
minced

1½ teaspoons smoked
paprika (pimentón de la
Vera), preferably hot, or
picante

¾ cup loosely packed
chopped fresh parsley

4 ounces goat cheese

Flaky sea salt, for serving

Escalivada is a Spanish dish of smoky grilled or roasted vegetables that hails from the Catalonia region of the country. Joe and I ordered it daily when we were in Barcelona, and each restaurant—and home, for that matter—has its own interpretation. The types of vegetables almost always remain the same, though: eggplant, bell peppers, and onions. Sometimes tomatoes are involved, too, but I like to let the former three take the spotlight, since tomatoes so often do.

My preferred way to enjoy escalivada is to pile it onto crusty bread, so this mash-up of the Catalan dish with the Italian bread salad panzanella is one I hope both countries will allow me. Tossing the smoky vegetables with torn, toasted bread not only adds bulk but lends textural contrast, as the vegetables are quite soft and silky on their own. Crumbled goat cheese isn't totally necessary, but the pockets of cool creaminess it lends are lovely, as is the brightness from the generous dose of chopped fresh parsley.

ARRANGE A RACK in the middle of the oven and heat the oven to 375°F. Line a rimmed baking sheet with parchment paper.

Use the tines of a fork or the tip of a paring knife to poke several shallow holes all over the eggplant (this helps it release steam while it roasts so it doesn't explode). Place the eggplant, bell peppers, and onion on the prepared baking sheet (no need to trim, peel, or cut them just yet). Drizzle with 1 tablespoon olive oil and rub to coat. Season all over with kosher salt and pepper. Roast until completely soft and blackened in spots, flipping the vegetables with tongs halfway through, about 1½ hours.

When the vegetables are roasted, remove from the oven, transfer to a rimmed cutting board, and let cool while you prepare the bread and vinaigrette.

Carefully remove the parchment paper from the baking sheet used to roast the vegetables and place the bread cubes on the now-empty baking sheet. Drizzle with 3 tablespoons olive oil and season with kosher salt and black pepper. Use tongs to toss and coat the bread, then spread into an even layer. Bake, tossing halfway through, until dry and pale golden brown, 6 to 8 minutes.

Meanwhile, in a large bowl, whisk together the remaining ¼ cup olive oil, the vinegar, garlic, smoked paprika, a generous pinch of kosher salt, and several grinds of black pepper until combined and emulsified.

Once the eggplant, peppers, and onion are cool enough to handle, peel the skins off and carefully cut each vegetable in half to release the heat trapped inside. Continue to let cool.

Once the bread cubes are toasted, let cool for 5 minutes.

Use a spoon to scrape the seeds from the bell peppers, then cut the peppers into roughly 1-inch pieces and add them to the bowl of vinaigrette. Cut the eggplant and onion into roughly 1-inch pieces and also add them to the bowl, along with the toasted bread cubes. Toss well to combine and coat in the vinaigrette and vegetable juices. Add the parsley and toss again.

Let rest at room temperature for at least 30 minutes and up to 4 hours, tossing occasionally, to distribute the juices and vinaigrette evenly. Before serving, taste and season with additional kosher salt and black pepper as needed. Crumble goat cheese over the salad, toss gently again, and sprinkle with a pinch of flaky sea salt.

Heirloom Tomato Salad alla Norma

SERVES 4 TO 6

6 tablespoons extra-virgin olive oil, divided, plus more as needed for frying

1 medium eggplant (about 1 pound), sliced into ½-inch-thick rounds

Kosher salt

3 tablespoons balsamic vinegar

1 small clove garlic, grated or minced

Red pepper flakes

1 (8-ounce) wedge ricotta salata cheese

2 pounds heirloom tomatoes (about 4 medium), cored and sliced crosswise ½ inch thick

Handful fresh basil leaves

One of my favorite summer pasta dishes is pasta alla Norma. The Sicilian classic features short, tubular, ridged pasta, silky fried eggplant, and fresh-basil-kissed tomato sauce, all finished off with a generous amount of grated, wonderfully dry and salty ricotta salata cheese. This is my interpretation in salad form. It's caprese-like, but swaps the mozzarella for slabs of ricotta salata and adds meltingly tender eggplant rounds to the equation. Definitely have crusty bread close by, as there are lots of savory juices to soak up here.

HEAT 4 TABLESPOONS olive oil in a large cast-iron or other heavy-bottomed skillet over medium-high heat until shimmering. Add as much eggplant as will fit in a single layer and fry, undisturbed, until golden brown on the bottom, 2 to 3 minutes. Flip and continue to fry until browned on the other side and tender, about 2 minutes more. Transfer to a paper towel–lined rimmed baking sheet and season with a generous pinch of salt. Repeat with the remaining eggplant, frying in batches and adding a generous glug of olive oil between each batch.

Whisk together the remaining 2 tablespoons olive oil, the balsamic vinegar, garlic, a generous pinch of salt, and a pinch of red pepper flakes in a small bowl until combined and emulsified.

Place the ricotta salata wedge on one of its flat sides and use a sharp chef's knife to cut it into thin triangular slices. Arrange the eggplant, tomato, and ricotta salata slices in an overlapping pattern on a serving platter. Drizzle with the vinaigrette. Tear the basil leaves into small pieces, if large; otherwise, keep them whole. Scatter the basil over the top and sprinkle with another pinch of red pepper flakes, if desired.

Stuffed Pepper Rice Salad

SERVES 4

Kosher salt

1 cup uncooked
long-grain brown rice,
rinsed well

4 tablespoons extra-
virgin olive oil, divided

½ pound hot or sweet
Italian sausage, casings
removed if using links

½ teaspoon fennel seeds

1½ teaspoons dried
oregano

4 tablespoons red wine
vinegar, divided

Freshly ground black
pepper

1 medium red bell pepper
(6 to 8 ounces), seeded
and diced

1 medium yellow bell
pepper (6 to 8 ounces),
seeded and diced

3 scallions (white and
green parts), thinly sliced

½ cup loosely packed
chopped fresh parsley

This hearty salad takes all the best components of classic stuffed peppers and deconstructs them into one very colorful bowl. Don't be tempted to swap the brown rice for white here. I prefer the former not just because it's more wholesome and has a deeper, nuttier flavor, but because it holds up better. It doesn't lose its chew when tossed in the herby red wine vinaigrette and stays al dente for hours and even days after, making this a salad that's worthy of picnics and make-ahead meals alike. And if you think brown rice is difficult to cook, well then say hello to your new favorite method. Cooking it like pasta is totally foolproof. There's no measuring of water needed and it comes out perfectly, with nicely separated grains, every single time.

BRING A LARGE pot of salted water to a boil over high heat. Add the rice to the boiling water and cook until tender, about 30 minutes.

Meanwhile, heat 1 tablespoon olive oil in a medium skillet over medium-high heat until shimmering. Add the sausage and cook, breaking it up with a wooden spoon, until browned and cooked through, 5 to 7 minutes. Set aside.

Lightly crush the fennel seeds using the bottom of a small, heavy saucepan or skillet, then place in a large bowl. Add the oregano, remaining 3 tablespoons olive oil, 2 tablespoons red wine vinegar, a few generous pinches of salt, and several grinds of pepper and whisk until combined and emulsified.

When the rice is ready, drain well and return it to the pot off the heat. Cover and set aside to steam for 10 minutes, then transfer to the bowl of vinaigrette. Toss to combine then set aside for 10 minutes to cool and allow the rice to absorb some of the vinaigrette.

Add the sausage and any juices in the pan, along with the bell peppers, scallions, parsley, and remaining 2 tablespoons vinegar. Toss well to combine. Taste and season with additional salt and pepper as needed. Serve warm or at room temperature.

Stone Fruit Salad with Rosé Vinaigrette

SERVES 4 TO 6

⅓ cup dry rosé wine

Finely grated zest of ½ medium lemon

Juice of ½ medium lemon (about 1½ tablespoons)

1 tablespoon honey

1 tablespoon extra-virgin olive oil

Kosher salt

1½ pounds stone fruit, such as peaches, nectarines, plums, and/ or apricots, pitted and cut into ½-inch-thick wedges

½ cup raw hazelnuts

Handful fresh mint leaves

Save the last glug of rosé from dinner to make this fresh and easy peak-summer fruit salad. I love using a combination of stone fruit, mostly because I have trouble picking favorites and a variety provides a rainbow of colors and flavors, but sticking with one yields great success, too. Choose a dry, mineral-driven rosé rather than one with sweetness for this salad, as it will become pleasantly syrupy but balanced when it mingles with the fruits' juices and honey.

ARRANGE A RACK in the middle of the oven and heat the oven to 350°F.

In a large bowl, whisk together the wine, lemon zest, lemon juice, honey, olive oil, and a pinch of salt until combined and emulsified. Add the stone fruit and toss to coat. Set aside while you toast the nuts, tossing occasionally, to allow the fruits to release some of their juices and mingle with the vinaigrette.

Meanwhile, spread the hazelnuts out on a rimmed baking sheet and toast in the oven, stirring halfway through, until fragrant and golden brown, 8 to 10 minutes. Let the nuts cool for 5 minutes, then wrap them in a clean kitchen towel and rub vigorously to remove as much of the skins as possible (don't worry about any skin that doesn't easily come off). Transfer the nuts to a cutting board and coarsely chop.

Tear the mint leaves into small pieces, if large; otherwise, keep them whole. Stir in the hazelnuts and scatter the mint over the top.

Grilled Watermelon and Lime with Olive Oil and Flaky Sea Salt

SERVES 4 TO 6

1 mini seedless watermelon (3 to 4 pounds), quartered and cut into 1-inch-thick slices

2 tablespoons packed light or dark brown sugar

2 medium limes, halved

Extra-virgin olive oil

Flaky sea salt, for serving

Wait! Don't turn that grill off just yet. One of the very best things you can do for yourself and the lucky ones you're feeding is to toss some summer fruit on those hot grates and make the perfect end to an uber-seasonal meal. Thick watermelon wedges are especially well-suited for the grill, where, when rubbed with a touch of brown sugar, they take on lovely grill marks. While you're at it, grill a couple of lime halves to concentrate their brightness. Finish off the wedges with a drizzle of grassy olive oil, a sprinkle of flaky sea salt, and a big squeeze of the warm citrus juice for a dead-simple dinner ending that magically feels pretty darn fancy.

HEAT AN OUTDOOR grill for high direct heat.

Sprinkle the watermelon slices evenly on both sides with brown sugar and rub to coat.

When the grill is hot, place the watermelon slices in a single layer. Add the lime halves, cut sides down. Grill, covered, until grill marks appear on both the watermelon and limes, flipping the watermelon halfway through, about 5 minutes total.

Arrange the grilled watermelon and limes on a serving platter. Drizzle with a bit of olive oil and sprinkle with a generous pinch of flaky sea salt. Serve immediately, squeezing the grilled limes over the watermelon.

Boozy Blueberries with Maple-Cinnamon Yogurt

SERVES 4

———

3 cups fresh blueberries (about 1½ pints)

2 tablespoons bourbon

2 tablespoons maple syrup, divided

Kosher salt

1 cup whole-milk plain Greek yogurt

2 teaspoons fresh lemon juice

1 teaspoon ground cinnamon

These blueberries almost feel like a wholesome breakfast—but the splash of bourbon gives them an edge. The caramel notes from the whiskey play nicely with the tart berries, while thick and creamy Greek yogurt dressed with nutty cinnamon and maple syrup catches all the sweet juices.

COMBINE THE BLUEBERRIES, bourbon, half the maple syrup, and a pinch of salt in a medium bowl. Let the mixture macerate at room temperature for 20 minutes, tossing and occasionally pressing down gently on some of the berries with the back of a spoon, to allow the blueberries to release some of their juices and the mixture to become syrupy.

When ready to serve, stir together the yogurt and lemon juice in a small bowl. Place the lemony yogurt in a shallow serving bowl and spread it out in a large, even circle with the back of a spoon. Drizzle with the remaining maple syrup and sprinkle with cinnamon. Spoon the blueberries and any juices that have accumulated over the yogurt and serve.

Fall

You might say fall has some big shoes to fill, seeing as it's pretty hard to compete with candy-sweet tomatoes, juicy corn, and summer's other riches. The season is hardly a wallflower, though. It's always a thrill to watch winter squash, hearty leafy greens, Brussels sprouts, and crisp apples roll in. The fun lies in finally cranking up your oven after months of intentionally trying to keep cool, and cozying up to salads that are a touch warmer, more comforting, and fit for sweater weather without being any less wholesome.

Cacio e Pepe Shaved Brussels Sprouts

SERVES 4 TO 6

1 pound Brussels sprouts, stem ends trimmed

Juice of 1 medium lemon (about 3 tablespoons)

Kosher salt

4 tablespoons extra-virgin olive oil

2 tablespoons red wine vinegar

½ teaspoon Dijon mustard

Freshly ground black pepper

2 ounces Pecorino Romano cheese, freshly grated (1 packed cup), divided

If you follow any food trends whatsoever, you'd think everyone's newfound love of Brussels sprouts would have petered out years ago. Yet, they prevail, which I think means the tiny brassicas are here to stay. I am a fan of Brussels sprouts every which way, but I especially love how their texture transforms when they're shaved paper-thin. You can do this by hand, with a mandoline, or, better yet, with the slicing blade of a food processor. The result is something slaw-like that you can take in so many directions, but you can never really go wrong by opting for the cheesy one.

This salad is inspired by the classic Roman dish of pasta tossed with *lots* of grated Pecorino Romano cheese and coarsely ground black pepper. It's salty, pungent, spicy, and totally moreish.

VERY THINLY SLICE the Brussels sprouts with a knife, mandoline, or a food processor fitted with the slicing blade and place them in a large bowl. Add the lemon juice and a generous pinch of salt. Massage with your hands to soften.

Whisk together the olive oil, vinegar, Dijon, and about 40 grinds of pepper in a small bowl until combined and emulsified.

Pour the dressing over the Brussels sprouts, add half of the Pecorino, and toss well to combine.

Taste and season with additional salt and pepper as needed, then garnish with the remaining Pecorino and several more grinds of pepper.

Rainbow Chard and Spiced Pepita Slaw

SERVES 4 TO 6

1 cup apple cider vinegar

1 cup water

2 teaspoons granulated sugar

Kosher salt

Freshly ground black pepper

1 medium bunch rainbow chard (about 8 ounces)

½ small red onion, very thinly sliced

4 tablespoons extra-virgin olive oil, divided

½ cup shelled pumpkin seeds (pepitas)

1 teaspoon chili powder, divided

½ teaspoon ground cinnamon, divided

Pinch cayenne pepper

Finely grated zest of 1 lime

Juice of 1 medium lime (about 2 tablespoons)

Flaky sea salt, for serving

Despite enjoying other leafy greens both cooked and raw—looking at you, kale and spinach—Swiss chard tends to fall strictly in the cooked camp. However, it's even more tender than kale, which means it's actually a wonderful contender for raw preparations. This simple slaw is the perfect example. It's also an exercise in reducing food waste, as instead of tossing the stems, they're quick-pickled and thrown right into the bowl for color and crunch.

BRING THE VINEGAR, water, sugar, 2 teaspoons kosher salt, and several grinds of pepper to a simmer in a small saucepan over medium heat. Remove from the heat.

Cut the stems off the chard and thinly slice. Add the chard stems and red onion to the saucepan and toss to coat. Set aside to pickle for 20 minutes while you toast the pepitas.

Heat 1 tablespoon olive oil in a medium skillet over medium heat until shimmering. Add the pepitas, ½ teaspoon chili powder, ¼ teaspoon ground cinnamon, the cayenne, and a big pinch of kosher salt and toast, tossing frequently, until golden and fragrant, 1 to 2 minutes. Transfer to a small bowl, add the remaining ½ teaspoon chili powder and ¼ teaspoon ground cinnamon, and toss to coat.

Once the chard stems and red onion are pickled, whisk together the lime zest, lime juice, 2 tablespoons of the pickling liquid, and the remaining 3 tablespoons olive oil in a large bowl until combined and emulsified.

Stack the chard leaves, very thinly slice them crosswise into ribbons, and place in the bowl of dressing. Remove the quick-pickled chard stems and red onion with a slotted spoon or drain through a fine-mesh strainer. Add to the bowl, along with half of the spiced pepitas. Toss to combine. Taste and season with additional kosher salt and pepper as needed.

Garnish with the remaining spiced pepitas and a big pinch of flaky sea salt.

Crunchy Cauliflower Salad with Tahini and Dates

SERVES 4

1 large head cauliflower (2 to 2½ pounds), cut into bite-sized florets

5 tablespoons extra-virgin olive oil, divided

1 teaspoon cumin seeds

Kosher salt

Freshly ground black pepper

⅓ cup raw almonds

¼ cup well-stirred tahini

Juice of 1 medium lemon (about 3 tablespoons)

3 tablespoons water, divided

1 tablespoon date syrup (see sidebar, opposite)

4 Medjool dates, pitted and coarsely chopped

3 scallions (white and green parts), thinly sliced

½ cup loosely packed chopped fresh parsley

As I am sure my husband can attest too, I like to sneak tahini into just about everything. I deeply admire the nutty complexity it brings to everything from soups to cookies, and of course, salad dressings. Here, a creamy tahini dressing latches on to the nooks and crannies of roasted cauliflower florets. Scallions and toasted almonds lend crunch, chopped dates provide chewy sweetness, and chopped parsley keeps forkfuls fresh. This is a salad that vies for your attention and is sure to draw some away from whatever you're serving it with.

ARRANGE 2 RACKS to divide the oven into thirds and heat the oven to 425°F.

Place the cauliflower florets on a rimmed baking sheet, drizzle with 3 tablespoons olive oil, and season with the cumin seeds, 1 teaspoon salt, and several grinds of pepper. Toss to coat and spread into an even layer.

Roast on the bottom rack, tossing halfway through, until the florets are tender and caramelized at the edges, 20 to 25 minutes. Meanwhile, toast the almonds and make the dressing.

Spread the almonds out on a small rimmed baking sheet and toast on the top rack, stirring halfway through, until fragrant and golden brown, 5 to 7 minutes. Let cool for 5 minutes, then roughly chop.

Whisk together the tahini, lemon juice, 1 tablespoon water, a generous pinch of salt, and several grinds of pepper in a large bowl until creamy and lightened in color. Add the date syrup, remaining 2 tablespoons olive oil and 2 tablespoons water, and whisk until smooth and pourable (it may seize during whisking, but this is normal; continue to whisk and it will smooth out).

Add the cauliflower, almonds, dates, scallions, and parsley to the bowl and toss to evenly coat in the dressing. Taste and season with additional salt and pepper as needed.

What Is Date Syrup?

Date syrup, also called date honey, date molasses, or silan, is simply dates that have been steamed and pressed into a thick, dark brown syrup. What I love about it is that its sweetness is more subdued and complex than honey or maple syrup, with toffee and butterscotch undertones. Soom is my go-to brand, which also happens to make my favorite tahini.

You can swap in half the amount of maple syrup for the date syrup in this recipe, but I highly encourage you to pick up a bottle to try. I love using it in homemade granola, drizzling it over pancakes, and placing a small bowl of it on a cheese board to pair with any kind of goat cheese.

Burnt Red Onion, Spinach, and Parmesan Salad

SERVES 4

2 medium red onions, cut into 1-inch wedges through the root

4 tablespoons extra-virgin olive oil, divided

Kosher salt

Freshly ground black pepper

1 tablespoon balsamic vinegar

1 tablespoon red wine vinegar

1 teaspoon Dijon mustard

5 ounces baby spinach (about 5 packed cups)

2 ounces Parmesan cheese, freshly shaved (about ⅔ cup), divided

Caramelized onions might get all the attention, but I think onions that have been roasted so deeply they come out of the oven blistered and burnt should receive just as much praise. This unassuming salad is inspired by one in Yotam Ottolenghi's book *Plenty More* that I tasted half a dozen years ago and have never been able to get out of my brain. Making pungent red onions the star is an unusual move. However, their flavor mellows under high heat, becoming a deeply savory match for sweet spinach and salty Parmesan.

ARRANGE A RACK in the middle of the oven and heat the oven to 450°F.

Place the onion wedges on a rimmed baking sheet. Drizzle with 2 tablespoons olive oil, season with ½ teaspoon salt and several grinds of pepper, and toss gently to coat, doing your best to keep the wedges intact. Spread out, one cut side down, in a single layer.

Roast the onions until very well browned underneath, 15 to 20 minutes. Carefully flip and continue to roast until the other side is well browned and the onions are very tender and burnt in spots, 10 to 15 minutes more.

Meanwhile, whisk together the remaining 2 tablespoons olive oil, the balsamic vinegar, red wine vinegar, Dijon, a generous pinch of salt, and several grinds of pepper in a large bowl until combined and emulsified.

Once the onions are roasted, add them to the bowl of vinaigrette along with the baby spinach and toss to combine (the onions may break apart a bit and the spinach will lightly wilt, both of which are okay). Add half of the shaved Parmesan and gently toss to combine. Taste and season with additional salt and pepper as needed. Garnish with the remaining shaved Parmesan.

Butter Lettuce Salad
with Creamy Walnut Dressing

SERVES 4

—

¼ cup raw walnuts

1 teaspoon Dijon mustard

1 clove garlic, smashed
and peeled

3 tablespoons white wine
vinegar

3 tablespoons extra-
virgin olive oil

Kosher salt

Freshly ground black
pepper

2 medium heads butter
lettuce (about 1 pound
total), such as Boston or
Bibb, torn into bite-sized
pieces

Butter lettuce's velvety texture and sweet flavor is so
lovely, it's really a shame to hide it under a pile of other
salad ingredients. Here, a creamy, but totally cream-free,
dressing made from toasted walnuts amplifies the greens'
butteriness.

ARRANGE A RACK in the middle of the oven and heat the oven
to 350°F.

Spread the walnuts in a single layer on a small rimmed
baking sheet and toast in the oven, stirring halfway through,
until fragrant and golden brown, 8 to 10 minutes. Let cool for
5 minutes.

Place the walnuts, Dijon, garlic, vinegar, olive oil, a generous
pinch of salt, and several grinds of pepper in a blender, preferably high-speed. Blend until completely smooth, stopping to
scrape down the sides of the blender as needed.

Place the lettuce in a large bowl, pour the dressing over
it, and toss to coat. Taste and season with additional salt and
pepper as needed.

Endive Salad with Pickled Raisin Vinaigrette

SERVES 4

1 teaspoon brown or yellow mustard seeds

½ cup golden raisins

½ cup water

½ cup white wine vinegar

1 teaspoon granulated sugar

Kosher salt

½ teaspoon red pepper flakes

4 medium heads Belgian endive (about 10 ounces total)

2 tablespoons extra-virgin olive oil

Freshly ground black pepper

If you're raisin averse, as so many are, I see you flipping the page right now. Hear me out, though: Golden raisins are a different breed. They're softer than their dried-out and shriveled dark brown equivalent, not to mention wonderfully tart and fruity rather than overly sweet. They're an ideal counterpart to bitter endive, especially when you give them a quick bath in brine so that they become pickled and plump. This is a simple salad that's much more than the sum of its parts.

PLACE THE MUSTARD seeds in a small saucepan over medium heat. Toast, shaking the pan frequently, until the seeds start to pop, about 2 minutes. Add the raisins, water, vinegar, sugar, 1 teaspoon salt, and the red pepper flakes and bring to a boil, stirring to dissolve the sugar and salt. Remove from the heat and set aside to pickle, uncovered, for 20 minutes.

Meanwhile, trim the browned ends off the bottom of each endive and separate into individual leaves, trimming the root as you go, until you get all the way to the core. Cut the cores in half lengthwise and place the leaves and cores in a large bowl.

Once the raisins are pickled, drain them and the mustard seeds through a fine-mesh strainer set over a bowl to catch the brine. Return the raisins and mustard seeds to the pan, off the heat. Add 2 tablespoons of the brine to the pan, discarding the rest. Add the olive oil and several grinds of black pepper and stir vigorously to combine and emulsify.

Scoop out a spoonful or two of the vinaigrette from the pan, doing your best to leave the raisins behind, and drizzle it over the endive. Gently toss to coat, then taste and season with additional salt and black pepper as needed. Pile half of the leaves on a serving platter or in a large shallow bowl with the cupped shape facing up. Spoon half of the remaining vinaigrette over the endive, making sure that some of the raisins catch in the little cups of the endive. Pile the remaining leaves on top and repeat with the remaining vinaigrette.

Harissa-Roasted Sweet Potatoes and Chickpea Salad

SERVES 4

¼ cup harissa

5 tablespoons extra-virgin olive oil, divided

2 pounds sweet potatoes (3 medium or 2 large), cut into 1-inch chunks

1 medium red onion, cut into 1-inch chunks

2 (15-ounce) cans chickpeas, drained and rinsed

Kosher salt

1 teaspoon cumin seeds

Freshly ground black pepper

Juice of 1 medium lemon (about 3 tablespoons)

½ preserved lemon, seeds and flesh removed, rind rinsed and thinly sliced (see sidebar, below)

⅔ cup loosely packed chopped fresh parsley

Here's a warm salad that makes a minimal mess. Toss chickpeas and chunks of sweet potato and red onion with fiery harissa, olive oil, and spices in a large bowl, dump it out onto a sheet pan to roast, then use that same bowl to whisk together a tangy preserved lemon dressing. You don't even need to reach for another bowl for serving the salad. Bring the whole sheet pan straight to the dinner table and let everyone dig right in.

ARRANGE A RACK in the middle of the oven and heat the oven to 425°F.

Whisk together the harissa and 3 tablespoons olive oil in a large bowl to combine. Add the sweet potatoes, red onion, chickpeas, cumin seeds, 1 teaspoon salt, and several grinds of pepper. Toss to coat, then spread the mixture out in a single layer on a rimmed baking sheet. Reserve the bowl (no need to wipe it out).

Roast, tossing halfway through, until the vegetables are tender and the chickpeas are crisp and browned in spots, 30 to 35 minutes.

Meanwhile, combine the lemon juice, remaining 2 tablespoons olive oil, and the preserved lemon rind in the reserved bowl.

Drizzle the roasted vegetables and chickpeas with the dressing, sprinkle with about three-quarters of the parsley, and gently toss on the baking sheet to combine. Transfer to a large serving bowl or serve right off the baking sheet, garnished with the remaining parsley.

All About Preserved Lemons

Wash, cut, and salt lemons, pack them in a jar topped off with lemon juice, let them pickle, and you have preserved lemons. They're a common ingredient in Middle Eastern and North African cuisine and pack a briny, intensely lemony punch that's unlike anything else. The preserving process

softens the citrus's rind so that it is entirely edible. Rinse well under cool water to remove excess salt, then chop the rind, flesh, or both, depending on the recipe. While you can make them, they're readily available in well-stocked grocery stores and Middle Eastern markets. Les Moulins Mahjoub is one such brand.

How else to use preserved lemons? Fold the chopped rind into hummus, toss the chopped rind and flesh with a garlic-and-olive oil–laced pasta, or blend both the rind and flesh into a paste to stir into soups and brush over fish and chicken before grilling or roasting.

Crispy Rice Salad
with Miso-Buttered Mushrooms

SERVES 4

———

5 tablespoons extra-virgin olive oil, divided

3 cups chilled day-old cooked long-grain brown or white rice, divided

3 tablespoons unsalted butter, divided

1 pound fresh shiitake mushrooms, stems removed, caps torn into bite-sized pieces

1 tablespoon low-sodium soy sauce or tamari

2 tablespoons white miso paste

4 large eggs

Kosher salt

Freshly ground black pepper

Juice of 1 medium lime (about 2 tablespoons)

1 tablespoon hot sauce, plus more for serving

1 cup loosely packed chopped fresh cilantro

2 tablespoons chopped fresh mint leaves

4 scallions (white and green parts), thinly sliced, divided

Any time you cook a pot of rice, make at least double what you need. This will leave you with enough leftovers for this crispy rice salad, which brings the crunchy greatness of fried rice to your salad bowl. Caramelized mushrooms glazed in miso butter plus a lacy fried egg mean umami-packed is an understatement here. Lots of fresh herbs, lime, and hot sauce keep every bite in balance.

HEAT 2 TABLESPOONS olive oil in a large nonstick or well-seasoned cast-iron skillet over medium heat until shimmering. Add half of the rice and cook, pressing the rice down occasionally, until the rice crackles and is browned and crispy on the bottom, about 3 to 5 minutes. Toss and continue to pan-fry until crispy all over, 2 to 3 minutes. Transfer to a large bowl. Repeat with another tablespoon of olive oil and the remaining rice.

Melt 1 tablespoon butter in the hot skillet. Add half of the mushrooms in a single layer (it's okay if a few overlap) and cook, undisturbed, until browned, about 5 minutes. Transfer to a plate.

Add another 1 tablespoon butter and repeat with the remaining mushrooms. Return the browned mushrooms on the plate to the skillet. Add the soy sauce, miso, and the remaining 1 tablespoon butter. Continue cooking, tossing to break up, melt, and disperse the miso and butter, until the mushrooms are tender and deeply browned all over, 4 to 5 minutes more. Transfer the mushrooms to the bowl of rice.

Drizzle the remaining 2 tablespoons olive oil into the skillet (no need to wipe it out) and heat until shimmering. Crack 4 large eggs into the skillet, season with salt and pepper, and let the eggs cook, undisturbed, until the whites are golden brown around the edges and set, and the yolks are runny, 2 to 4 minutes.

Meanwhile, add the lime juice, hot sauce, cilantro, mint, and half of the scallions to the bowl of mushrooms and rice and toss to combine. Taste and season with salt and pepper as needed. Divide the salad among individual serving bowls. Top each with a fried egg, the remaining scallions, and hot sauce.

Broccoli Fattoush
with Ricotta Salata Citronette

SERVES 4

2 pounds broccoli
(about 2 large heads)

5 tablespoons extra-
virgin olive oil, divided

Kosher salt

Freshly ground black
pepper

4 ounces ricotta salata
cheese

1 medium lemon

1 tablespoon red wine
vinegar

2 teaspoons ground
sumac

½ (7- to 8-ounce) bag
pita chips, broken into
bite-sized pieces
(about 1¾ cups)

1 cup loosely packed
chopped fresh parsley

2 medium scallions
(white and green parts),
thinly sliced

Aleppo pepper or Urfa
biber chile flakes, for
serving (optional)

Fattoush is a Middle Eastern salad made from stale pita bread that has been fried or toasted and tossed with lettuce, tomatoes, radishes, cucumbers, fresh herbs, and a tangy dressing. This fall twist swaps the summer vegetables for warm roasted broccoli. For the sake of convenience, I reach for store-bought pita chips so I don't have to bother frying. Plain or multigrain work, but I particularly like the extra wholesomeness and toasty, nutty flavor the latter bring. While ricotta salata might be Italian in origin, it lends a uniquely salty, milky quality to the tart citronette—this salad's citrus-forward vinaigrette.

Aleppo pepper and Urfa biber are two varieties of chile flakes that are less about heat than they are about earthy sweetness. Aleppo is a bit fruity, while Urfa biber is mildly smoky. Either are optional here, but a sprinkle adds one more dimension, if you'd like to play around.

ARRANGE A RACK in the middle of the oven and heat the oven to 425°F.

Trim ½ inch off the woody, dried-out bottom of the broccoli stems and discard. Cut the florets into bite-sized pieces and place on a rimmed baking sheet. Cut the stems into bite-sized pieces and add to the baking sheet.

Drizzle with 2 tablespoons olive oil, season with ½ teaspoon salt and several grinds of black pepper, and toss to coat. Spread out in an even layer. Roast, tossing halfway through, until tender and caramelized, 20 to 25 minutes.

Meanwhile, use a Microplane to finely grate about three-fourths of the ricotta salata into a large bowl (about a scant cup), reserving the rest. If some of the cheese breaks in the process, simply crumble it finely with your fingers and add it to the bowl. Use the Microplane to finely grate about half of the lemon rind into the bowl. Halve the lemon crosswise and squeeze the juice from both halves into the bowl (about 3 tablespoons). Add the

remaining 3 tablespoons olive oil, the red wine vinegar, sumac, and several grinds of black pepper to the bowl and stir vigorously to combine.

Once the broccoli is roasted, let cool for 5 minutes. Add the broccoli to the bowl of citronette and toss to coat. Add the pita chips, parsley, and scallions, then crumble the reserved piece of ricotta salata into the bowl and toss to combine. Taste and season with additional salt and black pepper as needed. Garnish with a couple of generous pinches of Aleppo pepper or Urfa biber chile flakes, if desired.

Fresh Fig, Prosciutto, and Barley Salad

SERVES 4

Kosher salt

1 cup pearl barley, rinsed and drained

4 tablespoons extra-virgin olive oil, divided

1 large shallot, thinly sliced

4 tablespoons sherry vinegar

1 teaspoon maple syrup

Freshly ground black pepper

6 thin prosciutto slices (about 3 ounces)

8 fresh figs, quartered (see Note)

3 ounces arugula (about 3 packed cups)

NOTE: Local is the way to go when it comes to fresh figs—those shipped from afar are picked before peak ripeness so that they can survive the long journey. However, depending on where you live, the grocery store might be your only option. If so, try to select figs that are heavy in the hand and quite soft.

The season for fresh figs is a short one, but it's one I eagerly await every year. When perfectly ripe, the fruit is so jammy and sweet it simply deserves to be eaten as is, out of hand. However, I can't help but play around, too. This grain salad shows off just how nicely figs pair with salty prosciutto, which is a common practice in Italy. It's a prime example of how opposites absolutely attract.

BRING A LARGE pot of salted water to a boil over high heat. Add the barley to the boiling water and cook until al dente (it should be tender but have a slight chew in the center), 25 to 30 minutes.

When the barley is ready, drain well and return it to the pot off the heat. Cover and set aside to steam for 10 minutes. Meanwhile, make the dressing.

Heat 1 tablespoon of the olive oil in a small skillet over medium heat. Add the shallot, season with a pinch of salt, and sauté until softened and golden, about 2 minutes. Transfer to a large bowl, add the remaining 3 tablespoons olive oil, the sherry vinegar, maple syrup, a generous pinch of salt, and several grinds of pepper, and whisk until combined and emulsified.

Add the barley to the bowl of dressing and toss to coat. Set aside for 5 minutes to cool and allow the grains to absorb some of the dressing.

Tear each of the prosciutto slices into a few pieces and add to the bowl of barley. Add the figs and arugula and toss to combine. Taste and season with additional salt and pepper as needed.

Boiled Cider–Glazed Roots with Spiced and Shredded Chicken

SERVES 4

½ gallon (2 quarts) unfiltered apple cider

1 pound boneless, skinless chicken thighs (about 4)

2 teaspoons garam masala

Kosher salt

¼ cup dry white wine

2 pounds root vegetables, such as carrots, parsnips, sweet potatoes, and beets, peeled and cut into 1-inch chunks

4 tablespoons extra-virgin olive oil, divided

Freshly ground black pepper

2 tablespoons apple cider vinegar

½ small shallot, finely chopped

3 ounces baby kale or arugula (about 3 packed cups)

¼ cup roasted and lightly salted shelled pistachios, coarsely chopped

This salad asks more of you than most of the others in the book, but I promise you'll be rewarded. Boiled cider is exactly what it sounds like: apple cider that's been simmered until so much of its liquid evaporates that it becomes thickly syrupy and honey-like. It's fall in a jar. This liquid gold is deeply sweet and concentrated with apple flavor. You can buy it online from Wood's Cider Mill, a small cider mill in Vermont, but if you're willing to take the (mostly hands-off) time to make it yourself, it's much cheaper. While it does require a few hours—it's best made in advance of preparing this salad—it's a pretty fun and easy cooking project.

Boiled cider can be used countless ways in the kitchen—see the sidebar on page 136 for some of my favorites—but start with this ultra-autumnal salad. It's a sticky, surprising glaze for roasted root vegetables, which are tossed with juicy, warm-spiced chicken and peppery greens. Reaching for a mix of your favorite roots like carrots, beets, and parsnips results in the most colorful bowl, but I've absolutely reached for just one, too, and not been disappointed.

A DAY OR TWO BEFORE, MAKE THE BOILED CIDER: Pour the apple cider into a medium saucepan and bring to a boil over high heat. Reduce the heat to medium-low and simmer, stirring occasionally to prevent the bottom of the pot from burning, until the cider has reduced significantly, to about 1 cup, and has become a syrup, 2 to 2½ hours. It should be the consistency of warm, very runny maple syrup, as it will continue to thicken to the consistency of honey off the heat. Transfer the boiled cider to a heatproof jar or container with an airtight lid and refrigerate.

Make the salad: Arrange 2 racks to divide the oven into thirds and heat the oven to 400°F. Remove the boiled cider from the fridge to warm to room temperature on the counter and line a rimmed baking sheet with parchment paper.

Sprinkle the chicken all over with the garam masala and ½ teaspoon salt, then place the thighs in an even layer in a broiler-safe 8 x 8-inch baking dish. Pour the white wine into the bottom of the baking dish and cover the dish tightly with aluminum foil. Transfer the dish to the top rack and braise until the chicken is cooked through, about 30 minutes. Meanwhile, prepare the vegetables.

Place the root vegetables on the prepared baking sheet. Drizzle with 2 tablespoons olive oil, sprinkle with 1 teaspoon salt and several grinds of pepper, and toss to evenly coat. Spread out in an even layer.

Roast the vegetables on the bottom rack for 20 minutes. Remove the baking sheet from the oven, drizzle the vegetables with ¼ cup boiled cider, and toss to combine. Spread back out in an even layer. Continue to roast until the vegetables are tender and caramelized, 15 to 20 minutes more. Return the remaining boiled cider to the fridge for another use.

Meanwhile, whisk together the remaining 2 tablespoons olive oil, the apple cider vinegar, shallot, a generous pinch of salt, and several grinds of pepper in a large bowl.

Once the chicken is cooked, shred the meat with 2 forks right in the baking dish and toss lightly in the pan juices.

Once the vegetables are cooked, remove them from the oven and turn the oven to broil.

Return the baking dish containing the chicken to the top rack and broil until the meat crisps around the edges, about 5 minutes.

Use tongs to transfer the chicken to the bowl of vinaigrette, then add 1 tablespoon of the pan juices; discard the rest. Add the roasted vegetables and greens. Taste and season with additional salt and pepper as needed. Serve warm, garnished with the pistachios.

A Handful of Other Ways to Enjoy Boiled Cider

Boiled cider will last for months in the refrigerator and is a great thing to keep on hand through the fall and winter months.

1. Use it in place of simple syrup in an old-fashioned cocktail to give it a seasonal twist.

2. Use it instead of honey in a hot toddy.

3. Toss apple pie or apple crisp filling with a spoonful to lend more concentrated flavor.

4. Stir it into coffee or tea instead of sugar.

5. Drizzle it on pancakes and waffles rather than maple syrup.

6. Replace some of the honey or maple syrup in your favorite granola recipe with boiled cider.

7. Top your morning yogurt or oatmeal with a generous drizzle.

Broiled Radicchio and Feta with Za'atar Vinaigrette

SERVES 4

2 medium heads radicchio (about 1½ pounds)

5 tablespoons extra-virgin olive oil, divided

Kosher salt

Freshly ground black pepper

1 (14- to 16-ounce) block or 2 (8-ounce) blocks feta cheese

2 tablespoons sherry vinegar

¼ cup golden raisins

1 tablespoon za'atar

2 teaspoons honey

Chopped fresh parsley, for serving

Aleppo pepper flakes, for serving (optional)

We're taught bitterness is a bad thing. However, just because it's a basic taste that's more foreign to our tongues than saltiness and sweetness doesn't mean it should be demonized. What I love about radicchio is, in fact, its inherent bitterness, which jolts your taste buds awake. The leafy vegetable is part of the chicory family, and while there are many different types in a beautiful array of shapes, colors, and sizes, the variety you'll most typically find is Chioggia, which looks like a small red cabbage.

This recipe shows off just how exciting bitterness can be. While wedges of radicchio are mellowed ever so slightly when broiled in the oven, there's still enough bite to contrast with the warm, salty chunks of feta. Both are tied together with a tangy vinaigrette that's sweetened with honey and raisins and made savory thanks to a spoonful of za'atar, a Middle Eastern spice blend of toasted sesame seeds, sumac, and some combination of dried oregano, thyme, and marjoram. I love finishing off with a sprinkle of Aleppo pepper—chile flakes that are tamer than your usual red pepper flakes and uniquely fruity and earthy—but even without it, this is one bold salad that will keep you on your toes.

ARRANGE A RACK in the top third of the oven (6 to 8 inches from the broiling element) and preheat the broiler to high.

Trim the dry end off each head of radicchio. Quarter lengthwise, through the core, and place the quarters on a rimmed baking sheet. Drizzle with 2 tablespoons olive oil and rub both sides of each wedge to coat, taking care to keep them intact. Lay them flat, cut side down, in a single layer. Sprinkle with ½ teaspoon salt and several grinds of pepper.

Drain the feta and pat dry. Cut the block(s) into eight even 2-inch squares (about 1 inch thick). Nestle the feta squares among the radicchio wedges and drizzle with 1 tablespoon olive oil. Broil until the radicchio is slightly wilted with charred edges and the feta has softened and browned on the top, about 10 minutes. Meanwhile, make the vinaigrette.

Combine the vinegar and raisins in a medium bowl and let rest for 5 minutes to allow the raisins to plump and soften. Add the remaining 2 tablespoons olive oil, the za'atar, honey, and a pinch of salt. Whisk until well combined and emulsified.

Carefully transfer the broiled radicchio and feta to a serving platter (or, better yet, serve it right off the baking sheet). Drizzle the za'atar vinaigrette over the top. Sprinkle with parsley and, if desired, Aleppo pepper.

Kale Chip Salad
with Smoky Turmeric Yogurt

SERVES 4

1 medium bunch curly
kale (about 8 ounces)

4 tablespoons extra-
virgin olive oil, divided

4 teaspoons low-sodium
soy sauce or tamari, divided

1 medium bunch lacinato
kale (about 8 ounces)

2 tablespoons rice vinegar

1 small clove garlic, grated
or minced

1 teaspoon grated peeled
fresh ginger

1 teaspoon honey

Freshly ground black
pepper

¼ cup raw sesame seeds

¼ cup unsweetened
shredded coconut

1 cup whole-milk plain
Greek yogurt

1 teaspoon smoked
paprika (pimentón de la
Vera), preferably hot, or
picante

¾ teaspoon ground
cumin

½ teaspoon ground
turmeric

1 teaspoon fresh lime juice

Kosher salt

Flaky sea salt, for serving

I'll be the first to agree with you that kale chips are hardly a substitute for actual chips. However, I do think they're fantastic in a salad. They lend big-time crunch, transforming a run-of-the-mill kale salad into a much more texturally interesting one.

This is a kale two ways sort of situation. You'll use two varieties of kale here: curly and lacinato (aka Tuscan or dinosaur). Curly kale is ideal for chips because its frilly edges crisp up exceptionally well in the oven. Lacinato kale is my favorite kale for any use beyond chips, though, because it's much more tender, which is especially important in salads. Here, it's the raw component of the salad. It's massaged and tossed in a ginger-garlic dressing before it joins up with the crunchy kale chips. Together, you get pleasant chew and brittle crunch in every forkful, which is made even more texturally fun by being dragged through the creamy spiced yogurt at the bottom of your bowl.

ARRANGE A RACK in the middle of the oven and heat the oven to 300°F. Strip the curly kale leaves from their stems and place in the bowl of a salad spinner. Rinse and spin dry, then pat dry with paper towels to ensure the kale is as dry as possible in order for it to crisp.

Tear the curly kale leaves into bite-sized pieces and place on a rimmed baking sheet. Drizzle with 1 tablespoon olive oil and 2 teaspoons soy sauce. Use your hands to massage the olive oil and soy sauce into the leaves to coat. Spread the kale into an even layer. Bake, tossing halfway through, until the kale is crisp, 18 to 20 minutes.

Meanwhile, strip the lacinato kale leaves from their stems and place in the bowl of the salad spinner. Rinse and spin dry, then tear into bite-sized pieces and place in a large bowl (no need to pat dry with paper towels). Using your hands, massage the leaves for about 1 minute or so, until they feel less stiff.

recipe continues . . .

Whisk together the remaining 3 tablespoons olive oil and 2 teaspoons soy sauce along with the rice vinegar, garlic, ginger, honey, and several grinds of pepper in a small bowl until combined and emulsified. Drizzle over the massaged kale and toss to coat.

Place the sesame seeds and shredded coconut in a small skillet and heat on medium. Toast, stirring frequently, until lightly golden brown and fragrant, about 5 minutes. Transfer to a small bowl.

Once the curly kale is crisp, transfer it to the bowl of dressed lacinato kale but do not toss just yet or the kale chips will lose their crunch.

Combine the yogurt, smoked paprika, cumin, turmeric, lime juice, and a pinch of kosher salt in a small bowl. Divide the yogurt among 4 shallow bowls or plates and spread it out in a large, even circle with the back of a spoon.

Gently toss the dressed kale and kale chips together. Taste and season with additional salt and pepper as needed. Divide the salad among the yogurt-lined bowls. Sprinkle generously with the toasted seeds and coconut, along with a pinch or two of flaky sea salt.

NOTE: You'll most likely have extra toasted sesame seeds and coconut. Store the mixture in an airtight container at room temperature for a few days and enjoy it sprinkled on freshly popped popcorn, avocado toast, and puréed vegetable soups.

Acorn Squash Wedge Salad

SERVES 4

2 medium acorn squash
(about 1½ pounds each)

5 tablespoons extra-
virgin olive oil, divided

1 tablespoon plus
2 teaspoons honey,
divided

Kosher salt

Freshly ground black
pepper

3 ounces thinly sliced
spicy salami, such as hot
soppressata, Calabrese
salami, or Spanish chorizo
(about 24 slices)

16 large fresh sage leaves

4 ounces hard aged
Gouda cheese

⅔ cup loosely packed
chopped fresh parsley

1 clove garlic, grated or
minced

2 tablespoons sherry
vinegar

When we think of cooking winter squash, our minds often go straight to incorporating sweet ingredients like brown sugar or cinnamon. Here, crispy crumbled salami chips, nutty aged Gouda, and earthy fried sage leaves prove squash can play just as well with salty, savory flavors, too. Though, to be sure, a little honey is snuck in for balance. This is a hearty salad that will keep your taste buds on their toes. Oh, and a friendly reminder that you can absolutely eat the squash skin! It gets nice and tender in the oven but holds on to a bit of its chew, which lends texture to every mouthful.

ARRANGE A RACK in the middle of the oven and heat the oven to 425°F.

Position 1 medium acorn squash on its side. Trim off both ends with a large, sturdy knife. Stand the squash upright on a flat end and cut in half lengthwise. Using a spoon, scrape out the seeds and any stringy bits. Cut each half into 4 quarters. Place the wedges upright, skin side down, in a baking dish large enough to fit the wedges nestled in a single layer (a 9 x 13-inch dish should do the trick) or on a rimmed baking sheet. Drizzle with 2 tablespoons olive oil, 1 tablespoon honey, 1 teaspoon salt, and several grinds of pepper.

Roast the squash until tender and caramelized at the edges, 40 to 45 minutes.

Meanwhile, heat a large skillet over medium heat. Add half of the salami slices to the pan in a single layer and cook until they curl and are lightly browned underneath, 1 to 2 minutes. Flip the slices and let cook until browned on the other side, about 1 minute more. Transfer the salami to a paper towel–lined plate. Repeat with the remaining salami.

Add 2 tablespoons olive oil to the skillet and heat until shimmering. Add the sage leaves and cook until crisp and lightly browned underneath, about 30 seconds. Use tongs to flip the leaves and let cook until crisp on the other side, about 30 seconds more. Transfer the leaves to the paper towel–lined plate.

recipe continues . . .

Once the salami and sage leaves are cool enough to handle, break them into small pieces and place in a medium bowl. Remove the rind from the Gouda and crumble the cheese into small pieces with the tines of a fork or a cheese knife, then add to the bowl. Add the parsley, garlic, sherry vinegar, and the remaining 1 tablespoon olive oil and toss to combine.

Once the squash is roasted, let it cool for a few minutes, then transfer the wedges to a serving platter. Spoon the cheese mixture over the wedges and drizzle with the remaining 2 teaspoons honey.

Hazelnut-Crusted Salmon Salad

SERVES 4

3/4 cup raw hazelnuts

1 small butternut squash (about 1½ pounds), peeled, seeded, and cut into 1-inch cubes

3 medium shallots, thinly sliced

4 tablespoons plus 1 teaspoon extra-virgin olive oil, divided

Kosher salt

Freshly ground black pepper

1 clove garlic, smashed and peeled

4 (6-ounce) skin-on or skinless salmon fillets

2 tablespoons Dijon mustard

2 tablespoons balsamic vinegar

1 tablespoon red wine vinegar

1 teaspoon maple syrup

1 large head red- or green-leaf lettuce (about 12 ounces), torn into bite-sized pieces

3/4 cup Castelvetrano olives, or another mild green olive, such as Cerignola, pitted and torn in half

There are plenty of ways to incorporate nuts into a dish, but using them in place of flour or bread crumbs to create a crunchy coating for chicken or fish is one of my favorites. Meaty salmon fillets are a great match with sweet, strongly flavored hazelnuts, which taste particularly of-the-season to me. The crusted, baked fillets would be lovely all on their own, but they become a meal when served over a salad of leaf lettuce and roasted butternut squash that has been tossed with buttery green olives and a simple maple-balsamic vinaigrette.

ARRANGE A RACK in the middle of the oven and heat the oven to 425°F.

Spread the hazelnuts out on a small rimmed baking sheet and toast in the oven, stirring halfway through, until fragrant and golden brown, 5 to 7 minutes. Let cool for 5 minutes, then wrap the toasted hazelnuts in a clean kitchen towel and rub vigorously to remove as much of the skins as possible (don't worry about any skin that doesn't easily come off). Transfer the nuts to the bowl of a food processor fitted with the blade attachment.

Place the squash and shallots on a rimmed baking sheet. Drizzle with 2 tablespoons olive oil, season with ½ teaspoon salt and several grinds of pepper, and toss to coat. Arrange in a single layer and roast for 20 minutes.

Meanwhile, add the garlic and 1 teaspoon olive oil to the food processor with the hazelnuts. Pulse until very coarsely ground, about 25 pulses. Transfer to a wide, shallow bowl or pie plate.

Pat the salmon fillets dry with a paper towel and season all over with salt and pepper. Brush the Dijon mustard on the tops of the fish. Place the fish, mustard side down, in the chopped hazelnuts and press firmly to coat so that they adhere. Place the fish, nut side up, on a large plate. If there are any nuts left, use your hands to press them onto the fish.

recipe continues . . .

Remove the baking sheet from the oven. Flip the squash, then push the vegetables to fill one half of the baking sheet. Place the salmon fillets, crust side up, on the other half of the baking sheet.

Return the baking sheet to the oven and continue to roast until the squash is tender and caramelized and the salmon is cooked through and flakes easily, 8 to 12 minutes, depending on the thickness of your fillets. An instant-read thermometer inserted into the middle of the thickest fillet should read 120°F to 130°F for medium-rare or 135°F to 145°F, if you prefer your salmon more well-done.

Meanwhile, whisk together the remaining 2 tablespoons olive oil, the balsamic vinegar, red wine vinegar, maple syrup, a generous pinch of salt, and several grinds of pepper in a large bowl until combined and emulsified.

Add the lettuce and toss to coat. Scrape the squash and shallot mixture into the bowl, add the olives, and gently toss to combine. Divide among 4 shallow bowls or plates and top each with a salmon fillet.

Dukkah-Crusted Delicata Squash and Goat Cheese Salad

SERVES 4

¼ cup raw hazelnuts

¼ cup shelled pistachios (either raw and unsalted or roasted and lightly salted)

2 tablespoons sesame seeds

2 teaspoons coriander seeds

2 teaspoons cumin seeds

Kosher salt

2 medium delicata squash (about 2 pounds), halved lengthwise, seeded, and cut into ¾-inch-thick slices

4 tablespoons extra-virgin olive oil, divided, plus more for serving

1 tablespoon honey

Freshly ground black pepper

2 tablespoons sherry vinegar

1 tablespoon finely chopped shallot

½ teaspoon Dijon mustard

5 ounces baby mustard greens or arugula (about 5 packed cups)

4 ounces goat cheese, crumbled (about 1 cup)

½ small lemon, for serving

Dukkah is an Egyptian nut, seed, and spice blend that's equal parts savory, sweet, zesty, and crunchy. When I had the chance to visit Egypt a handful of years ago, I popped into countless spice shops with the hope of bringing home authentic dukkah as a souvenir. I quickly learned it's a spice blend that's typically prepared at home rather than premade, and everyone has their own iteration. Cumin, coriander, sesame seeds, and nuts like walnuts, hazelnuts, and pistachios are common, but really, that's just the starting point. Fennel seeds, caraway seeds, cayenne, and even dried mint can sometimes make an appearance.

Stateside, dukkah has gained in popularity. You'll find versions at various spice shops and even Trader Joe's, but since my trip, I've learned that it's cheaper, tastier, and just as easy to make yourself. Here, my take on it encrusts sweet half-moons of roasted delicata squash, which is arguably my favorite winter squash, as it slices easily and there's no need to peel it.

Do yourself a favor and make a double or triple batch of the dukkah; you can store it in an airtight container at room temperature for a week or two, and combine it with good olive oil for the ultimate dip for crusty bread or warm pita, which is its most traditional use. It's also great sprinkled on eggs or roasted vegetables, or used as a crust for baked chicken or fish.

ARRANGE A RACK in the middle of the oven and heat the oven to 400°F. Line a rimmed baking sheet with parchment paper.

Place the hazelnuts, pistachios, sesame seeds, coriander seeds, and cumin seeds in a small skillet. Toast over medium heat, shaking the skillet frequently, until the nuts and seeds are fragrant and golden in spots, about 3 minutes. Immediately transfer to the bowl of a food processor fitted with the blade attachment.

recipe continues . . .

Add a generous pinch of salt to the food processor and pulse until the mixture is coarsely chopped, about 25 pulses.

Place the delicata squash in a large bowl, drizzle with 2 table-spoons olive oil and the honey, season with ½ teaspoon salt and several grinds of pepper, and toss to coat.

Transfer the dukkah from the food processor to the bowl of squash and toss to coat. Place the squash slices in a single layer on the prepared baking sheet, pressing the dukkah firmly on the slices to adhere. If there is any dukkah left in the bottom of the bowl, sprinkle it over the squash. Roast until the squash is tender and the coating is browned, 30 to 35 minutes.

Meanwhile, whisk together the remaining 2 tablespoons olive oil, the sherry vinegar, shallot, Dijon, a generous pinch of salt, and several grinds of pepper in a large bowl until combined and emulsified.

Once the squash is roasted, add the greens to the bowl of vinaigrette and toss to coat. Add half of the goat cheese and toss gently to distribute. Taste and season with additional salt and pepper as needed.

Spread out the dressed greens on a serving platter. Top with the squash and remaining goat cheese. Garnish with a drizzle of olive oil and a squeeze of lemon juice.

Brown-Buttered Brussels Sprouts and Orecchiette Salad

SERVES 4

4 ounces pancetta, diced

2 tablespoons unsalted butter

1 tablespoon honey

3 cloves garlic, grated or minced

1 pound Brussels sprouts, trimmed and halved

Kosher salt

Freshly ground black pepper

12 ounces dried orecchiette pasta

2 tablespoons balsamic vinegar

Pasta salad is a summer staple, to be dished out at picnics, potlucks, and barbecues. Who says we need to pack it away after Labor Day, though? This warm pasta salad is decidedly autumnal. Brussels sprouts get extra caramelized when they're roasted in honey-sweetened brown butter and the flavorful grease left over from crisping up pancetta. Toss them with al dente orecchiette, inky balsamic vinegar, and those crunchy, salty bits of pancetta, and you have a pasta salad that rivals any you'd eat in July.

ARRANGE A RACK in the middle of the oven and heat the oven to 425°F.

Place the pancetta in a small skillet set on medium heat. Cook, stirring occasionally, until the fat has rendered and the pancetta is crispy and browned, 5 to 7 minutes. Use a slotted spoon to transfer the pancetta to a paper towel–lined plate.

Add the butter to the skillet to melt. Continue cooking, swirling the pan occasionally, until the butter has a nutty aroma and is a toasty-brown color, about 3 minutes. Remove from the heat, add the honey and garlic, and stir continuously until the honey melts.

Place the Brussels sprouts on a rimmed baking sheet and drizzle with half of the brown butter mixture. Season with ½ teaspoon salt and several grinds of pepper and toss to coat. Arrange the Brussels sprouts in a single layer, cut side down.

Roast the Brussels sprouts, stirring halfway through, until the leaves are dark brown and crisp and the undersides of the sprouts are browned, 20 to 25 minutes total. Meanwhile, bring a large pot of salted water to a boil over high heat.

Add the pasta to the boiling water and cook until al dente, about 9 minutes or according to the package instructions. Drain the pasta, then transfer to a large bowl. Drizzle the remaining half of the brown butter sauce over the pasta, add the roasted Brussels sprouts, pancetta, and balsamic vinegar, and toss to combine. Taste and season with additional salt and pepper as needed.

Bourbon-Baked Apples with Cinnamon Toast Croutons

SERVES 4

———

2 large tart apples,
such as Honeycrisp,
Gala, or Pink Lady
(12 to 16 ounces total)

4 tablespoons unsalted
butter, melted, divided

2 tablespoons packed
light or dark brown sugar,
divided

1 tablespoon plus
½ teaspoon ground
cinnamon, divided

Freshly grated nutmeg
(optional)

¼ cup bourbon

¼ cup hot water

2 to 3 slices brioche
or challah bread, cut
into ½-inch cubes
(about 2 cups)

Kosher salt

Vanilla ice cream,
for serving

This playful dessert ensures your entire kitchen will be filled with the heady aroma of spiced baked fruit and all the cozy, sweater-weather feels that come with it. A big splash of bourbon in the bottom of the baking dish prevents the apples from burning in the oven, and, as it reduces, combines with the butter and brown sugar to become a nutty pan sauce for the fruit. Topping each warm apple half with a scoop of vanilla ice cream is an obvious finishing touch, but it's the scattering of sweet and crunchy cinnamon toast–inspired croutons that surprise and delight.

ARRANGE 2 RACKS to divide the oven into thirds and heat the oven to 375°F.

Cut the apples in half and cut out the cores using a sharp paring knife or spoon (a grapefruit spoon works perfectly). Place the halves cut side up in an 8 x 8-inch baking dish.

Drizzle 2 tablespoons melted butter on top of the apple halves. Sprinkle with 1 tablespoon brown sugar, ½ teaspoon ground cinnamon, and a few grates of nutmeg, if desired.

Pour the bourbon and hot water into the bottom of the baking dish and cover the dish tightly with aluminum foil. Bake on the top rack for 30 minutes. Carefully uncover and continue to bake until the apples are tender and the liquid has reduced slightly, 10 to 15 minutes more.

Meanwhile, place the bread cubes on a rimmed baking sheet. Drizzle with the remaining 2 tablespoons melted butter. Sprinkle with the remaining 1 tablespoon brown sugar, 1 tablespoon ground cinnamon, and a pinch of salt. Toss to coat, rubbing the sugar and cinnamon into the bread. Spread out in an even layer and bake on the bottom rack, tossing halfway through, until golden brown, 8 to 10 minutes.

Place each apple half in an individual serving bowl and drizzle generously with the pan juices. Top each with a scoop of ice cream and a handful of the brioche croutons.

Blistered Grapes
with Ricotta and Salted Honey

SERVES 4

1 pound seedless red grapes

1 tablespoon extra-virgin olive oil

1 teaspoon chopped fresh rosemary leaves

Kosher salt

3 tablespoons honey

¼ teaspoon apple cider vinegar

¼ teaspoon flaky sea salt

1 cup high-quality whole-milk ricotta cheese (about 8 ounces)

It wasn't until I was in college, living steps from the Union Square Greenmarket in New York, that I realized grapes are truly a fall fruit—and the best are nothing like what you can buy year-round at the store. There, vendors sold boxes piled with grapes in a million shades of purple, red, and green. The fruit was so sweet, bees would hover around the clusters, and the crisp air was perfumed with the most luscious scent.

This simple dessert celebrates the fall fruit that deserves just as much attention as apples. If you can get your hands on local grapes, you'll indeed be rewarded, but even if a grocery store bag is your only option, you'll be left with memorable results. That's because the grapes are roasted slowly so their flavor concentrates and they become caramelized and blistered. Their warm sweetness is perfect all on its own, but it's even better when contrasted with cool, creamy dollops of ricotta and a liberal drizzle of salted honey.

ARRANGE A RACK in the middle of the oven and heat the oven to 425°F.

Remove the stems from the grapes and place the grapes in an 8 x 8-inch baking dish. Drizzle with the olive oil, sprinkle with the rosemary and a pinch of kosher salt, and gently shake the dish to evenly coat the grapes and spread them out in a single layer. Roast until the grapes are soft, blistered, and have begun to release some of their juices, about 30 minutes. Meanwhile, make the salted honey.

Whisk the honey, vinegar, and flaky sea salt together in a small bowl to combine.

Dollop ricotta in generous spoonfuls on a serving platter. Use a spoon to transfer the grapes and any accumulated juice to the open spaces on the platter. Drizzle salted honey over the top and serve.

Persimmon and Gingered Pecan Salad

SERVES 4

¼ cup packed light or dark brown sugar

2 teaspoons ground ginger

½ teaspoon kosher salt

¼ teaspoon ground cinnamon

1 large egg white

1 cup pecan halves

Juice of 1 medium orange (about ¼ cup)

1 teaspoon maple syrup

1 teaspoon orange liqueur, such as Grand Marnier or Cointreau (optional)

4 firm but ripe medium Fuyu persimmons, peeled, cored, and cut into ½-inch wedges

½ cup pomegranate seeds, divided

NOTE: You'll make more gingered pecans than you need for this recipe, but their crunchy sweetness hardly makes that a problem. They'll stay fresh stored in an airtight container at room temperature for a couple of weeks and can be snacked on out of hand, sprinkled on yogurt, added to other salads, or even used as an ice cream topping.

When it comes to fall fruit, persimmons are truly an underdog. However, they really do deserve so much more attention. The two most common varieties are Hachiya and Fuyu. Hachiya persimmons are oblong and acorn-shaped. They're astringent and inedible when firm. Once they're totally soft, they are peeled and only their pulpy flesh is spooned out, often to be used in baked goods as you would use pumpkin purée. Fuyu persimmons are round, squat, and edible when firm or soft, with or without the peel. The latter are the easiest to love, in my opinion, especially when perfectly ripe—they're ridiculously juicy and candy-like in sweetness. Here, slices star in a jewel-toned bowl made complete with spicy candied pecans, tart pomegranate seeds, and a citrusy dressing.

ARRANGE A RACK in the middle of the oven and heat the oven to 350°F. Line a small rimmed baking sheet with parchment paper.

Whisk together the brown sugar, ginger, salt, and cinnamon in a medium bowl to combine, breaking up any large clumps of sugar.

Beat the egg white in a medium bowl until frothy. Add the pecans and toss to coat. Use your hands or a slotted spoon to lift the nuts out of the bowl and into the spice mixture, leaving any excess egg white behind. Toss to coat evenly in the spice mixture then spread out in a single layer on the prepared baking sheet.

Bake, tossing occasionally to separate the nuts and prevent them from burning, until the nuts are dry, toasted, and fragrant, 15 to 20 minutes. Remove from the oven and let cool on the baking sheet while you prepare the salad.

Whisk together the orange juice, maple syrup, and orange liqueur (if using) until combined. Add the persimmons and toss to coat.

Roughly chop about half of the toasted pecans (reserve the rest for snacking—see Note) and add them to the bowl of persimmons, along with half of the pomegranate seeds. Toss to combine. Garnish with the remaining pomegranate seeds.

Winter

Winter is as much a season for salads as any other, despite what you might think. Sure, farmers markets are whittled down and so much of the produce at the grocery store is shipped in from sunnier locales, but there are still plenty of riches to be had. Most are humble, such as cabbage, cauliflower, potatoes, and other root vegetables, and simply need a little extra TLC to coax out their inherent goodness and transform them into something more showstopping than you'd ever imagine.

Roasted Garlic Kale Salad with Parmesan Rind Croutons

SERVES 4

———

FOR THE ROASTED GARLIC VINAIGRETTE

1 head garlic

3 tablespoons plus 1 teaspoon extra-virgin olive oil, divided

Kosher salt

2 tablespoons red wine vinegar

1 teaspoon Dijon mustard

Freshly ground black pepper

FOR THE SALAD

2 small or 1 large bunch lacinato or flat-leaf kale (about 12 ounces), stems removed and leaves torn into bite-sized pieces

Extra-virgin olive oil, for greasing

4 ounces Parmesan cheese rinds (about 2 medium rinds)

Kosher salt

Freshly ground black pepper

While buying pre-grated Parmesan cheese is convenient, you're always better off keeping your fridge stocked with a block of it to grate yourself. It's richer in flavor and free of strange anti-clumping agents, for certain, but the greatest gift is the rind that comes with that block of Parmesan. Whatever you do, once the block is whittled down, don't throw the rind away. Simmer it in a pot of soup, tomato sauce, or even store-bought broth, and its umami-rich goodness will improve the flavor tenfold.

The ultimate party trick, though, is to broil bite-sized squares of Parmesan rind so they become crouton-like: They'll puff like balloons and become golden brown and crisp. This transformation happens almost instantaneously, so definitely keep a close eye on them while they are in the oven. The crunchy garnish is what ensures this isn't just another kale salad.

MAKE THE ROASTED GARLIC VINAIGRETTE: Arrange one rack in the middle of the oven and another rack in the top third of the oven (6 to 8 inches from the broiling element) and heat the oven to 400°F.

Peel off the papery outer layers of the head of garlic, keeping just a few firm inner layers in order to keep the head intact. Slice ¼ to ½ inch off the top crosswise to expose the cloves. Place the garlic, cut side up, in the middle of a piece of aluminum foil. Drizzle with 1 teaspoon olive oil, sprinkle with a pinch of salt, and wrap loosely in the aluminum foil. Roast directly on the middle rack until the cloves are deeply golden and caramelized, about 1 hour.

Unwrap the garlic and set aside until it's cool enough to handle. Squeeze the cloves out of their skins into a small bowl. Mash with a fork until you have a mostly smooth purée (a few lumps are okay). Add the remaining 3 tablespoons olive oil, the

vinegar, Dijon, a generous pinch of salt, and several grinds of pepper, and whisk until combined and emulsified.

Make the salad: Place the kale in a large bowl. Using your hands, massage the leaves for about a minute or so until they feel less stiff. Whisk the vinaigrette once or twice more to ensure it is emulsified, then drizzle about half of it over the kale and toss to coat. Set aside while you make the croutons.

Preheat the broiler to high. Line a rimmed baking sheet with aluminum foil. Very lightly grease the foil by drizzling it with a little olive oil and rubbing with your fingers to evenly coat.

Cut the Parmesan rind into ½-inch squares and spread them out, rind side down, on the prepared baking sheet. Broil on the top rack until puffed and golden brown, about 2 minutes, then use tongs to flip the pieces and broil until golden brown on the other side, about 1 minute more.

Drizzle the remaining vinaigrette over the kale and toss to coat. Taste and season with additional salt and pepper as needed. Sprinkle with the Parmesan rind croutons and serve.

Bittersweet Radicchio Salad

SERVES 4

½ cup raw walnuts

3 tablespoons extra-virgin olive oil

Juice of 1 medium orange (about ¼ cup)

2 teaspoons pomegranate molasses

1 teaspoon Dijon mustard

½ teaspoon light or dark brown sugar

1 small clove garlic, grated or minced

Kosher salt

Freshly ground black pepper

2 small heads radicchio (about 12 ounces total), preferably a mix of varieties like Chioggia and Castelfranco

Flaky sea salt, for serving

The first time I picked up a bottle of pomegranate molasses, also called pomegranate syrup, I used it for a single recipe and then left it sitting untouched because I wasn't sure what to do with the rest. Don't make my mistake. It's a wonderful ingredient to keep in the kitchen and brings magic to so many things (see my suggestions in the sidebar on page 166). Look for it in Middle Eastern markets, online, and at Whole Foods. Here, the sweet-tart syrup counters the natural bitterness of radicchio. The strong flavors play off each other to result in a vibrant winter salad.

Chioggia is the standard grocery store variety of radicchio, but if you're lucky enough to come across other varieties like butter-yellow, red-speckled Castelfranco, tall and pointy Treviso, and pale pink Rosa del Veneto, a combination makes for a beautiful bowl.

ARRANGE A RACK in the middle of the oven and heat the oven to 350°F.

Spread out the walnuts in a single layer on a small rimmed baking sheet and toast in the oven, stirring halfway through, until fragrant and golden brown, 8 to 10 minutes. Let cool for 5 minutes.

Meanwhile, whisk together the olive oil, orange juice, pomegranate molasses, Dijon, brown sugar, garlic, a generous pinch of kosher salt, and several grinds of pepper in a large bowl.

Trim the ends off the radicchio. Tear the radicchio leaves into bite-sized pieces and add them to the bowl. Toss to evenly coat in the vinaigrette. Taste and season with additional salt and pepper as needed.

Coarsely chop the walnuts, add to the bowl, and toss lightly to distribute. Sprinkle with a generous pinch of flaky sea salt before serving.

Seven More Ways to Use Pomegranate Molasses

1. Stir a little into club soda or tonic water for a refreshing nonalcoholic drink.

2. Combine it with olive oil and orange juice and use it as a marinade for chicken, lamb, swordfish, or salmon.

3. Dress up store-bought hummus with a drizzle.

4. Swap it in for some of the honey or maple syrup in your favorite granola recipe.

5. Use it to make muhammara, a traditional Middle Eastern roasted red pepper and walnut dip.

6. Drizzle roasted vegetables (especially Brussels sprouts, eggplant, carrots, and sweet potatoes) with a bit as soon as they come out of the oven.

7. Toss a bowl of sweet summer berries with a spoonful.

Wilted Cabbage and Warm Shallot Salad

SERVES 4

3 tablespoons extra-virgin olive oil

1 tablespoon unsalted butter

4 medium shallots, thinly sliced

2 cloves garlic, thinly sliced

Kosher salt

Freshly ground black pepper

½ medium (2- to 3-pound) head green cabbage

2 tablespoons balsamic vinegar

2 tablespoons red wine vinegar

2 teaspoons Dijon mustard

2 teaspoons honey

2 ounces Gruyère cheese, freshly shaved (about ⅔ cup), divided

Cabbage might just be the humblest vegetable around. It sits patiently among all the other winter vegetables, often getting ignored. It's inexpensive and unassuming. When it's taken home, though, it gives and gives. A head of cabbage lasts forever in your refrigerator's crisper drawer and can be transformed into a countless number of cozy, wholesome dishes. This simple recipe is inspired by retro warm spinach salads, but instead of spinach, thinly sliced green cabbage is the star. It's tossed with a warm caramelized shallot dressing and paired with lots of nutty shaved Gruyère cheese for a winter salad that's modest in the best way.

HEAT THE OLIVE oil and butter in a medium skillet over medium heat until the butter melts. Add the shallots and garlic, season with a generous pinch of salt and several grinds of pepper, and cook, stirring frequently and reducing the heat if the shallots and garlic start to burn, until the shallots are very soft, caramelized, and deep golden brown, about 15 minutes.

Meanwhile, quarter, core, and thinly slice the cabbage crosswise. Place in a large bowl. Sprinkle with a generous pinch of salt and massage with your hands to soften.

Once the shallots have caramelized, remove the skillet from the heat and whisk in the balsamic vinegar, red wine vinegar, Dijon, and honey.

Pour the shallot mixture over the cabbage and toss to coat and wilt. Taste and season with additional salt and pepper as needed. Add half of the shaved Gruyère and toss to distribute the cheese. Garnish with the remaining shaved Gruyère.

Escarole and Sunchoke Salad

SERVES 4 TO 6

½ cup white wine vinegar

½ cup water

1 teaspoon granulated sugar

Kosher salt

Freshly ground black pepper

4 small sunchokes or Jerusalem artichokes (about 6 ounces), very thinly sliced

1½ ounces Pecorino Romano cheese, freshly grated (¾ packed cup), divided

4 tablespoons extra-virgin olive oil

Juice of 1 medium lemon (about 3 tablespoons)

2 teaspoons Dijon mustard

1 medium head escarole (about 1 pound)

This is my take on a favorite salad—a simple bowl of escarole and shaved sunchokes tossed in a lemony Pecorino Romano dressing—from a restaurant I frequented in New York City. Sunchokes, also known as Jerusalem artichokes, are a late fall and winter root vegetable that are tubular and knobby—a lot like fresh ginger root. Their skin is thin enough that there's no need to peel them—just scrub them well—and their creamy white flesh is earthy, sweet, and nutty. When roasted, their texture is almost potato-like, while they are crispy and juicy, similar to water chestnuts or jicama, when thinly shaved and eaten raw.

Unfortunately, sunchokes can have a bit of a gassy effect on certain individuals because they contain a type of fiber called inulin that our bodies can't digest. Inulin is found in lots of other foods, such as asparagus, bananas, garlic, and onions, so its effects are subjective, but some people do feel them. Pickling sunchokes, however, as I've done here, converts some of the inulin to a more digestible form. It also leaves them wonderfully tangy and extra crunchy.

BRING THE VINEGAR, water, sugar, 1 teaspoon salt, and several grinds of pepper to a simmer in a small saucepan over medium heat. Remove from the heat. Add the sunchokes to the saucepan and toss to coat. Set aside to pickle for 20 minutes, swirling the pot occasionally to distribute the sunchokes throughout the brine.

Whisk together half of the grated Pecorino, the olive oil, lemon juice, Dijon, a generous pinch of salt, and several grinds of pepper in a large bowl.

Once the sunchokes are pickled, drain them and add to the bowl of dressing. Remove and discard any very tough outer dark green or brown leaves from the head of escarole. Tear the remaining leaves into bite-sized pieces. Add the escarole to the bowl with the pickled sunchokes and dressing and toss to coat. Taste and season with additional salt and pepper as needed. Garnish with the remaining grated Pecorino and several more grinds of pepper.

Bok Choy Salad with Ginger-Grapefruit Vinaigrette

SERVES 4

1 small pink or red grapefruit

2 tablespoons extra-virgin olive oil

1 tablespoon maple syrup

2 teaspoons grated peeled fresh ginger

2 teaspoons white miso paste

Freshly ground black pepper

1 pound baby bok choy (3 or 4)

Kosher salt

¼ cup roasted salted peanuts, roughly chopped (optional)

Baby bok choy is a vegetable I've always cooked until I realized it might be even more tasty raw. It's wonderfully crisp and tender, making this a bright, palate-cleansing salad that's a respite alongside heavier winter fare. Miso lends a touch of salty savoriness to the grapefruit dressing, and freshly grated ginger adds spice, though neither overwhelms it. Crunchy bok choy and tart, juicy citrus are front and center here.

TRIM THE TOP and bottom from the grapefruit so that it rests flat on the cutting board, then cut away the peel and pith, following the curve of the fruit. Working over a large bowl, use a paring knife to cut between one of the grapefruit segments and the connective membrane then slice along the adjacent membrane until the cuts meet, releasing the segment into the bowl. Repeat with the remaining segments. Squeeze the spent membrane over the bowl to release its juices, then discard the membrane.

Add the olive oil, maple syrup, ginger, miso, and several grinds of pepper to the bowl of grapefruit juice and segments. Stir vigorously to combine, dissolve the miso, and emulsify, being careful not to break apart the segments too much in the process.

Trim off the browned, dried ends of the bok choy. Halve each bok choy lengthwise, then slice both the white and green parts crosswise into roughly ½-inch ribbons. Add to the bowl and toss to combine. Taste and season with salt and additional pepper as needed. Garnish with chopped peanuts, if desired.

Marinated Golden Beet and Provolone Salad

SERVES 4

4 large loose golden beets
(1½ to 2 pounds)

3 tablespoons extra-
virgin olive oil

2 tablespoons red wine
vinegar

Finely grated zest of
½ medium lemon

Juice of ½ medium lemon
(about 1½ tablespoons)

2 sprigs fresh rosemary

1 clove garlic, grated or
minced

1 teaspoon Dijon mustard

¼ teaspoon red pepper
flakes

Kosher salt

Freshly ground black
pepper

1 (4-ounce) block sharp
provolone cheese, cut
into ½-inch cubes
(about 1 cup)

¼ cup loosely packed
chopped fresh parsley

1 tablespoon capers,
rinsed well (if salt-
packed) and drained
(chopped, if large)

Here's a beet recipe for the beet averse. I say this as some-
one who very much agrees that they generally taste like
dirt. However, I am continually trying to figure out how
to tame their overpoweringly earthy flavor, and I do believe
this salad solves the problem. Golden beets are milder
and sweeter than red beets, and when bathed in a garlicky
rosemary-and-lemon-infused marinade, they take on an
Italian-antipasto-like quality. Tossing cubes of sharp provolone and briny capers into the bowl especially make that
happen. It's a magical way to bring beets to the table that
I can absolutely get behind.

ARRANGE A RACK in the middle of the oven and heat the oven
to 400°F.

Wash and scrub the beets thoroughly (no need to dry them),
then individually wrap each beet loosely in aluminum foil. Place
on a rimmed baking sheet. Roast until the beets are knife-
tender, 50 to 60 minutes. Meanwhile, make the marinade.

Place the olive oil, red wine vinegar, lemon zest, lemon juice,
rosemary sprigs, garlic, Dijon, red pepper flakes, a generous
pinch of salt, and several grinds of black pepper in a small saucepan and warm over medium-low heat until very fragrant, about
3 minutes. Remove from the heat and let cool for a minute.

Place the provolone cheese in a large bowl, pour the marinade over it, and toss to coat. Toss the cheese occasionally while
the beets roast to evenly coat in the marinade.

Once the beets are done, remove from the oven, carefully
unwrap, and set aside until cool enough to handle but still
warm, about 15 minutes. Working with one beet at a time, rub
the skin off gently with a paper towel. The skin should peel
away easily; if it doesn't, the beets likely need to cook for a little
longer. Cut the peeled beets into ½-inch-thick wedges, add
them to the marinade, and toss to coat. Marinate for 20 minutes, tossing occasionally.

Remove and discard the rosemary sprigs. Stir in the parsley and capers. Taste and season with additional salt and black
pepper as needed.

Blackened Broccoli Rabe Caesar

SERVES 4

4 large eggs plus 1 raw egg yolk, divided

¼ loaf good sourdough or country-style bread, torn into roughly 1-inch pieces (about 2 cups)

6 tablespoons extra-virgin olive oil, divided

Kosher salt

Freshly ground black pepper

6 oil-packed anchovy fillets

1 clove garlic, smashed and peeled

1 teaspoon Dijon mustard

Juice of ½ medium lemon (about 1½ tablespoons)

1 tablespoon red wine vinegar

2 tablespoons freshly grated Parmesan cheese, plus more for serving

1½ pounds broccoli rabe (about 2 bunches)

½ teaspoon red pepper flakes, divided

One of the best ways to tone down strong flavors is to introduce them to equally powerful ones. That's exactly the tactic here. Broccoli rabe is naturally quite bitter, sometimes overwhelmingly so. Introduce it to a punchy Caesar dressing, amplified by garlic, anchovies, and Parmesan, and they are forced to play as equals. I top this salad with a soft-boiled egg for protein, but grilled or pan-seared steak, chicken, or salmon would also pair nicely and round out the bowls.

ARRANGE 2 RACKS to divide the oven into thirds and heat the oven to 375°F. Let the eggs rest on the counter to take the chill off from the fridge—this will help prevent them from cracking when boiled.

Place the torn bread on a rimmed baking sheet. Drizzle with 1 tablespoon olive oil, season with salt and black pepper, and toss to coat. Spread out in an even layer, transfer to the bottom rack, and bake, tossing halfway through, until golden brown, about 15 minutes.

Meanwhile, bring a medium pot of water to a boil. Fill a medium bowl with ice and water.

Mash the anchovies and garlic clove into a rough paste with a mortar and pestle. (Alternatively, you can very finely chop and mash both together into a paste on a cutting board and transfer to a small bowl, but a mortar and pestle really works best.) Stir in the Dijon, lemon juice, vinegar, and several grinds of black pepper. Add the egg yolk and 2 tablespoons olive oil and stir vigorously until combined and emulsified. Stir in the grated Parmesan. Set the dressing aside.

Once the croutons are toasted, transfer them to a bowl or plate. Increase the oven temperature to 425°F.

Trim about ½ inch off the ends of the broccoli rabe and cut into roughly 2-inch pieces. Place half on the now-empty baking sheet and the remaining half on another rimmed baking sheet. Drizzle each baking sheet of broccoli rabe with 1½ tablespoons olive oil and season with ¼ teaspoon salt, several grinds of black pepper, and ¼ teaspoon red pepper flakes. Toss to coat, then spread out in a single layer.

Roast, rotating the pans from top to bottom halfway through, until the stems are tender and the leaves are charred in spots, 10 to 15 minutes.

Meanwhile, carefully lower the eggs into the boiling water with a slotted spoon. Boil, uncovered, for 7 minutes for soft-boiled eggs with jammy, but not runny, yolks. Transfer the eggs to the ice bath with a slotted spoon and chill until cold, about 5 minutes.

Drizzle the broccoli rabe with the dressing and toss to coat on the baking sheet. Taste and season with additional black pepper as needed. Divide among individual serving bowls or plates.

Remove the eggs from the ice bath, then peel and halve lengthwise. Arrange an egg on each salad, top with the croutons, and garnish with lots of grated Parmesan and black pepper.

French Onion–Stuffed Mushrooms with Bitter Greens

SERVES 4

---

2 tablespoons unsalted butter

1½ pounds yellow onions (about 3 medium), thinly sliced

1 tablespoon fresh thyme leaves

Kosher salt

Freshly ground black pepper

4 large portobello mushrooms

5 tablespoons extra-virgin olive oil, divided

¼ cup dry white wine

2 tablespoons plus 1 teaspoon sherry vinegar, divided

4 ounces Gruyère cheese, grated (about 1 cup)

⅓ cup fresh or panko bread crumbs

1 clove garlic, grated or minced

1 teaspoon Dijon mustard

6 ounces bitter greens (about 6 packed cups), such as arugula, radicchio, frisée, dandelion greens, or a combination, torn into large bite-sized pieces, if needed

I ate a lot of stuffed portobello mushrooms during my days as a vegetarian. I was in college and single—portobellos were cheap and perfectly portioned for one. The caps are endlessly versatile. Stuff them with cheese, beans, sautéed greens, cooked grains, roasted vegetables, or even mashed squash or potatoes. Of all the iterations I've worked my way through, though, these French onion soup–inspired stuffed mushrooms win first prize. An abundance of jammy caramelized onions is loaded into the portobello caps before they're topped with nutty Gruyère cheese and baked. The results are so umami-packed, they beg to be served atop a simple, vinaigrette-dressed salad for balance. A smattering of toasted bread crumbs mimics the crispy bits of the cozy, classic soup.

ARRANGE A RACK in the top third of the oven and heat the oven to 400°F.

Melt the butter in a large skillet over medium heat. Add the onions, thyme, ½ teaspoon salt, and several grinds of pepper. Cook, stirring frequently, until the onions have reduced by more than half and are very soft and deep golden brown, 28 to 30 minutes. Reduce the heat if the onions start to burn.

Meanwhile, remove and discard the stems from the mushrooms. Use a spoon to gently scrape out and discard the gills to make room for the filling. Brush the mushroom caps on both sides with 2 tablespoons olive oil and season with ½ teaspoon salt and several grinds of pepper. Place the mushrooms on a rimmed baking sheet, stem side down, and roast until they just begin to soften, about 10 minutes.

Once the onions are caramelized, pour in the wine. Scrape up any browned bits on the bottom of the pan and continue to stir until the wine has evaporated, about 1 minute. Remove the pan from the heat and stir in 1 teaspoon vinegar.

recipe continues . . .

Once the mushrooms are just softened, remove the baking sheet from the oven and flip the mushrooms over with a flat spatula. Divide the caramelized onions evenly among the mushroom caps, then sprinkle with the Gruyère.

Roast until the mushrooms are tender and the cheese just starts to melt, 5 to 7 minutes. Switch the oven to broil on high and broil until the cheese browns, 2 to 3 minutes.

Meanwhile, heat 1 tablespoon olive oil in a small skillet over medium heat until shimmering. Add the bread crumbs, garlic, a pinch of salt, and a few grinds of pepper. Toast, stirring frequently, until golden brown, 3 to 5 minutes. Transfer to a small bowl.

Whisk together the remaining 2 tablespoons olive oil, 2 tablespoons vinegar, the Dijon, a generous pinch of salt, and several grinds of pepper in a large bowl. Add the greens and toss to coat. Taste and season with additional salt and pepper as needed. Divide among individual shallow bowls or plates.

Top each serving with a stuffed mushroom and sprinkle with the toasted bread crumbs.

Smashed Potato and Chorizo Sheet Pan Salad

SERVES 4

1½ pounds baby red or Yukon Gold potatoes

Kosher salt

5 tablespoons extra-virgin olive oil, divided

1 pound fresh Mexican chorizo, casings removed if using links

4 medium scallions, white and pale green parts cut into 1-inch pieces and dark green parts thinly sliced, divided

Finely grated zest of 1 medium lime

Juice of 1 medium lime (about 2 tablespoons)

1 small clove garlic, grated or minced

½ medium romaine lettuce heart, sliced into thin ribbons

4 ounces queso fresco cheese, crumbled (about 1 cup)

This unconventional salad isn't shy. Smashed baby potatoes soak up the spicy juices from Mexican chorizo as they roast together harmoniously on a sheet pan. The two become a dinner salad once they're tossed with shredded lettuce and scallions, drizzled with a puckering lime vinaigrette, and finished with plenty of salty cheese crumbles.

Queso fresco is a semisoft Mexican cheese, similar to feta in milky-tangy flavor and crumbly texture, that can be found in rounds in the cheese section of most grocery stores. If you can't find it, a mild feta can be substituted.

PLACE THE POTATOES and 1 tablespoon salt in a large saucepan. Cover with cool water by 1 inch, then bring to a boil over high heat. Reduce the heat to medium and simmer until the potatoes are easily pierced with a knife, 10 to 15 minutes. Drain in a colander and rinse under cold water to cool slightly. Set aside in the colander to let the skins dry.

Meanwhile, arrange 2 racks to divide the oven into thirds and heat the oven to 450°F. Drizzle a rimmed baking sheet with 2 tablespoons olive oil.

Once the potatoes are cool enough to handle, transfer them to the prepared baking sheet and shake the baking sheet to coat the potatoes in the oil. Press down on each potato with the bottom of a measuring cup or drinking glass until it splits and flattens to about ¼ inch thick.

Pull the chorizo into bite-sized clumps with your hands and scatter them in the open spaces between the potatoes. Scatter the white and pale green parts of the scallions on top. Drizzle with 1 tablespoon olive oil and season with ½ teaspoon salt and several grinds of pepper.

Roast on the bottom rack until the bottoms of the potatoes are golden brown, 20 to 25 minutes. Switch the oven to broil on high, transfer the baking sheet to the top rack, and broil until the tops of the potatoes are golden brown, 3 to 4 minutes more.

Meanwhile, whisk together the lime zest, lime juice, garlic, the remaining 2 tablespoons olive oil, a generous pinch of salt, and several grinds of pepper in a small bowl.

Scatter the lettuce and thinly sliced dark green parts of the scallions over the potatoes and chorizo. Drizzle with the vinaigrette and toss gently on the baking sheet to lightly wilt the lettuce and coat everything in the vinaigrette. Taste and season with additional salt and pepper as needed. Sprinkle the crumbled queso fresco on top and serve the salad right off the baking sheet. (Alternatively, transfer to a large serving bowl.)

Burst Cherry Tomato and Garlic Bread Caprese Salad

SERVES 4

___

3 pints cherry tomatoes (about 1¾ pounds or 6 cups)

3 tablespoons extra-virgin olive oil

4 sprigs fresh rosemary

Kosher salt

Freshly ground black pepper

½ loaf good sourdough or country-style bread, torn into roughly 1-inch pieces (about 4 cups)

2 tablespoons unsalted butter, melted

3 cloves garlic, grated or minced

1 pound fresh mozzarella cheese

1 tablespoon balsamic vinegar

Flaky sea salt, for serving

Red pepper flakes, for serving (optional)

It's hard to beat a caprese salad made with the juiciest summer tomatoes. You can, however, riff on it spectacularly in the winter by using cherry tomatoes, which hold on to their flavor out of season, especially when it's coaxed out in the oven. Roast the tomatoes with plenty of olive oil and a few sprigs of rosemary to become warm and luscious, then spoon them over torn fresh mozzarella for a cold-weather twist on caprese that's sure to be a new favorite. If you're not convinced, the buttery garlic bread croutons that are scattered over the whole mess should do the trick.

ARRANGE 2 RACKS to divide the oven into thirds and heat the oven to 375°F.

Place the cherry tomatoes, olive oil, rosemary, ½ teaspoon kosher salt, and several grinds of black pepper in a 9 x 13-inch baking dish. Gently shake the dish to evenly coat the tomatoes and spread in a single layer. Transfer to the top rack and roast, giving the baking dish another shake halfway through, until the tomatoes are blistered, caramelized, and beginning to burst, 35 to 40 minutes. Meanwhile, prepare the garlic bread croutons.

Place the torn bread on a rimmed baking sheet. Drizzle with the melted butter. Sprinkle with the garlic, season with kosher salt and black pepper, and toss to coat, rubbing the garlic into the bread. Spread out in an even layer, transfer the pan to the bottom rack, and bake, tossing the garlic bread halfway through, until golden brown, about 15 minutes.

Tear the mozzarella into large, two- or three-bite pieces and arrange them on a serving platter.

Remove and discard the rosemary sprigs from the roasted tomatoes. Drizzle the tomatoes with the balsamic vinegar and toss to coat. Spoon the tomatoes into the open spaces on the platter and drizzle some of the juices that remain in the pan over both the tomatoes and mozzarella. Scatter the garlic bread over the top. Sprinkle with a pinch of flaky sea salt and, if desired, red pepper flakes.

Honey-Mustard Parsnip and Pancetta Salad

SERVES 4

2 pounds parsnips

5 tablespoons extra-virgin olive oil, divided

Kosher salt

Freshly ground black pepper

4 ounces pancetta, diced

4 cloves garlic, thinly sliced

3 tablespoons apple cider vinegar

1 tablespoon honey

1 tablespoon Dijon mustard

1 tablespoon whole-grain mustard

4 ounces arugula (about 4 packed cups)

Parsnips rarely get their time in the spotlight. While the root vegetable might look like a white carrot, the flavor is totally its own. Parsnips are sweet, with a uniquely nutty spiciness. This intensifies when they are roasted and caramelized in a hot oven. Here, a honey-mustard dressing showcases their sweetness, while salty bits of pancetta and a finishing shower of crunchy garlic chips counter it.

ARRANGE A RACK in the middle of the oven and heat the oven to 425°F.

Peel and trim the parsnips. If they are very long, cut them in half crosswise, and if they are more than 1 inch thick, cut them in half lengthwise; otherwise, leave them whole. Place on a rimmed baking sheet, drizzle with 2 tablespoons olive oil, season with ½ teaspoon salt and several grinds of pepper, and toss to coat. Spread the parsnips into a single layer and sprinkle the pancetta in the spaces between the parsnips. Roast for 15 minutes.

Meanwhile, pour the remaining 3 tablespoons olive oil into a small skillet, then arrange the sliced garlic in a single layer in the oil. Turn the heat to medium. Cook, stirring frequently, until the garlic is golden brown, 3 to 5 minutes. Use a slotted spoon to transfer the garlic to a paper towel–lined plate to drain and sprinkle with salt. Reserve the skillet of garlic-infused oil.

Flip the parsnips, then roast until the parsnips are tender and the edges are charred and crispy, and the pancetta is rendered and browned, 15 to 20 minutes more.

Meanwhile, add the apple cider vinegar, honey, Dijon, whole-grain mustard, a generous pinch of salt, and several grinds of pepper to the skillet of garlic-infused oil and whisk until combined and emulsified.

Once the parsnips and pancetta are roasted, drizzle with half of the dressing and toss to coat on the baking sheet.

Place the arugula in a medium bowl, drizzle with the remaining dressing, and toss to coat. Taste and season with additional salt and pepper as needed, then spread out on a serving platter. Arrange the parsnips and pancetta on top and garnish with the garlic chips and several grinds of pepper.

Sicilian Cauliflower "Couscous" Salad

SERVES 4

1 medium head cauliflower (1½ to 2 pounds), cut into bite-sized florets

⅓ cup golden raisins

2 tablespoons white wine vinegar

2 tablespoons extra-virgin olive oil

1 small yellow onion, finely chopped

¼ teaspoon saffron threads

3 oil-packed anchovy fillets

¼ cup pine nuts

½ teaspoon fennel seeds

¼ teaspoon red pepper flakes, plus more for serving

1 (15-ounce) can chickpeas, drained and rinsed

Kosher salt

⅓ cup loosely packed chopped fresh parsley

Finely grated zest of ½ medium lemon

Juice of ½ medium lemon (about 1½ tablespoons)

Freshly ground black pepper

This saffron-tinged salad is inspired by *pasta chi vruoccoli arriminati*, a classic Sicilian pasta dish that literally translates to "pasta that is mixed with cauliflower." The dish is a study in how opposites attract. You might not think cauliflower can commingle with salty anchovies, sweet golden raisins, licorice-y fennel seeds, and red pepper flakes all at the same time, yet they're harmonious together. There's no actual pasta in this twist. Instead, cauliflower is blitzed into couscous-like crumbles, then sautéed with a flavor-packed combination of good things.

If you'd like to save a step, you can skip making the cauliflower couscous and swap in about 4 cups of fresh or frozen store-bought cauliflower rice. If using frozen, break up any large clumps and toss it directly into the hot skillet—no need to thaw.

PLACE HALF OF the cauliflower in the bowl of a food processor fitted with the blade attachment. Pulse until the cauliflower is finely chopped and resembles couscous, about 20 pulses. Transfer to a medium bowl and repeat with the remaining cauliflower.

Combine the raisins and vinegar in a small bowl and set aside for the raisins to plump and soften while you prepare the cauliflower couscous.

Heat the olive oil in a large skillet over medium heat until shimmering. Add the onion and sauté until softened and translucent, 3 to 5 minutes. Crumble the saffron into the skillet and add the anchovies, pine nuts, fennel seeds, and red pepper flakes. Sauté until the anchovies have dissolved and the pine nuts are golden, 1 to 2 minutes. Stir in the cauliflower couscous and chickpeas. Season with ½ teaspoon salt and sauté until the cauliflower is tender and the chickpeas are warmed through, 3 to 5 minutes. Remove from the heat.

Add the raisins and vinegar, parsley, lemon zest, and lemon juice to the cauliflower mixture and toss to combine. Taste and season with black pepper and additional salt as needed. Transfer to a serving bowl, if desired, and garnish with a bit more red pepper flakes.

Fregola Salad with Smothered Italian Greens

SERVES 4

Kosher salt

1½ pounds hearty greens, such as kale, mustard greens, or Swiss chard (about 2 bunches)

4 tablespoons extra-virgin olive oil, divided, plus more for serving

1 small yellow onion, finely chopped

1 sprig fresh rosemary

3 tablespoons tomato paste

½ (6- to 7-ounce) log dry Italian salami (such as Toscano or finocchiona), halved lengthwise, casing removed, and sliced crosswise into ¼-inch-thick half-moons

4 cloves garlic, thinly sliced

1 teaspoon fennel seeds

½ teaspoon red pepper flakes, plus more for serving

½ cup dry white wine

3 tablespoons balsamic vinegar, divided

1½ cups fregola sarda, or Israeli (pearl) couscous

Freshly ground black pepper

High-quality whole-milk ricotta cheese, for serving

If you're familiar with Israeli (or pearl) couscous, fregola is the Italian version—Sardinian, to be exact. Like Israeli couscous, it's made with semolina flour and water and rolled into small pearl-like balls. The distinction is that fregola—also called fregola sarda or fregula—is pre-toasted, which lends color and wonderfully nutty flavor to the spherical pasta. Fregola is also rolled by hand, whereas Israeli couscous is made by machine.

Seeking out fregola at your local Italian market, specialty store, or online is worth it if you've never had it before, though Israeli couscous can be used here in a pinch. It's also well worth picking up high-quality dry Italian salami, as the better the salami, the richer in flavor the greens will be.

BRING A LARGE pot of salted water to a boil over high heat.

If using kale, remove and discard the stems. If using mustard greens or chard, simply trim the thick bottom stems and discard. Coarsely chop the greens. Rinse in a colander but do not dry.

Heat 2 tablespoons of the olive oil over medium heat in a large, high-sided sauté pan with a lid until shimmering. Add the onion and rosemary sprig and sauté until the onion is softened and translucent, 3 to 5 minutes. Add the tomato paste and sauté until the paste has deepened in color, about 1 minute. Add the salami, garlic, fennel seeds, and red pepper flakes and sauté until fragrant, about 1 minute. Pour in the wine, scrape up any browned bits on the bottom of the pan, and continue to stir until the wine has evaporated, about 1 minute.

Add the greens a few handfuls at a time, stirring after each addition so that they start to wilt, until all the greens are added. Stir in 1 tablespoon vinegar and ½ teaspoon salt. Reduce the heat to low, cover, and cook, stirring occasionally, until the greens are very tender, about 10 minutes.

Meanwhile, add the fregola sarda to the boiling water and cook until tender, about 10 minutes.

Whisk together the remaining 2 tablespoons olive oil, 2 tablespoons vinegar, a generous pinch of salt, and several

grinds of black pepper in a large bowl until combined and emulsified.

Once the greens are cooked, remove and discard the rosemary sprig and add the greens to the bowl of dressing. When the fregola is cooked, drain through a fine-mesh strainer and add to the bowl. Toss to combine. Taste and season with additional salt and black pepper as needed. Garnish each serving with a generous dollop of ricotta, a drizzle of olive oil, and more red pepper flakes.

Warm Spiced Lentil and Wild Rice Salad

SERVES 4 TO 6

1 cup dried French green lentils, picked over and rinsed

1 cup uncooked wild rice, rinsed well

4 cups water

Kosher salt

5 tablespoons extra-virgin olive oil, divided, plus more for serving

1 medium yellow onion, finely chopped

2 teaspoons ground cumin

2 teaspoons ground coriander

1 teaspoon smoked paprika (pimentón de la Vera), preferably hot, or picante

¾ teaspoon ground turmeric

½ teaspoon ground cinnamon

Freshly ground black pepper

3 tablespoons sherry vinegar

¾ cup loosely packed chopped fresh cilantro

½ cup loosely packed chopped fresh parsley

Whole-milk plain Greek yogurt, for serving (optional)

I grew up surrounded by a large Lebanese population, which meant hummus, tabbouleh, and kibbeh were household words. My dad would often stop at the Lebanese market on his way home from work to gather a collection of things for an easy midweek dinner. Mujadara was one of my very favorites. The dish of rice, lentils, and caramelized onions is wholesome and filling. This salad is loosely inspired by it but a far cry from the classic iteration. Wild rice and peppery green lentils take the place of white rice and earthy brown lentils, and lots of heady spices like smoked paprika, cumin, turmeric, and cinnamon are tossed in. A slew of chopped fresh herbs and a big splash of sherry vinegar keep things bright. Dollop servings with cool and creamy Greek yogurt and you can rest assured you're eating well.

PLACE THE LENTILS and wild rice in a medium pot and add the water and 1 teaspoon salt. Bring to a boil over high heat, then lower the heat to maintain a gentle simmer. Cover and simmer until the liquid has been absorbed, the lentils are quite tender, and the rice is chewy and some of the grains have burst open, 45 to 55 minutes.

Meanwhile, heat 2 tablespoons olive oil in a medium skillet over medium heat until shimmering. Add the onion, cumin, coriander, smoked paprika, turmeric, cinnamon, a generous pinch of salt, and several grinds of pepper. Cook, stirring frequently, until the onion is very soft and caramelized, 28 to 30 minutes. Reduce the heat if the onion starts to burn.

Remove the onions from the heat and pour in the vinegar, scraping up any browned bits on the bottom of the pan with a wooden spoon. Add the remaining 3 tablespoons olive oil and stir to combine and emulsify.

Once the rice and lentils are cooked, transfer to a large bowl. Add the onion mixture, cilantro, and parsley, and toss to combine. Taste and season with additional salt and pepper as needed. Garnish each serving with a dollop of Greek yogurt, if desired, and a drizzle of olive oil.

Caramelized Fennel and White Bean Salad

SERVES 4

4 tablespoons extra-virgin olive oil, divided

2 medium fennel bulbs, trimmed, quartered, and thinly sliced (reserve ½ cup of the feathery fronds)

2 teaspoons fresh thyme leaves

Kosher salt

Freshly ground black pepper

3 tablespoons red wine vinegar

1 tablespoon Dijon mustard

1 clove garlic, grated or minced

2 (15-ounce) cans white beans, such as cannellini, drained and rinsed

½ cup dry white wine

½ small lemon, for serving

Onions aren't the only vegetable you can caramelize. Thinly sliced fennel takes on the same deep golden color and softened texture when cooked slowly on the stovetop. Fennel's strong anise flavor also mellows when caramelized, and the vegetable becomes sweeter and more approachable. When tossed with creamy white beans and a simple garlicky dressing, the result is a balanced, satisfying bowl.

HEAT 2 TABLESPOONS olive oil in a large skillet over medium heat until shimmering. Add the fennel and thyme, season with ½ teaspoon salt and several grinds of pepper, and cook, stirring occasionally and reducing the heat if the fennel starts to burn, until soft and caramelized, about 25 minutes.

Meanwhile, whisk together the remaining 2 tablespoons olive oil, the vinegar, Dijon, garlic, a generous pinch of salt, and several grinds of pepper in a large bowl. Add the white beans and toss to coat.

Once the fennel is caramelized, pour in the wine. Scrape up any browned bits on the bottom of the pan and continue to stir until the wine has evaporated, about 1 minute. Transfer the fennel to the bowl of beans and toss to combine.

Coarsely chop the reserved fronds, add them to the bowl, and toss to combine. Taste and season with additional salt and pepper as needed. Serve warm or at room temperature, squeezing the lemon over the salad just before serving.

Seared Slaw with Honey and Sun-Dried Tomato Baked Cheese

SERVES 4 TO 6

1 small (1- to 1½-pound) or ½ medium (2- to 3-pound) head red cabbage, tough outer leaves removed

Kosher salt

Freshly ground black pepper

3 tablespoons extra-virgin olive oil, divided

⅓ cup oil-packed sun-dried tomatoes (about 2 ounces), drained, patted dry, and coarsely chopped

1 tablespoon honey, plus more for serving

2 teaspoons chopped fresh oregano leaves

2 tablespoons plus 1 teaspoon balsamic vinegar, divided

¼ teaspoon red pepper flakes

¼ cup loosely packed chopped fresh parsley

2 scallions (white and green parts), thinly sliced

1 (9-ounce) wheel Harbison cheese, or other 8- to 9-ounce wheel bloomy-rind cheese, such as Brie or Camembert

Here's permission to eat a whole wheel of cheese for dinner. Baked bloomy-rind cheeses like Brie and Camembert are a retro appetizer that never really went out of style, especially around the holidays. Why reserve all that gooey luxury for festivities when you can turn it into a cozy winter meal? The key is to bring a little balance to the situation. Here, it's a warm red cabbage slaw. In keeping with the retro vibes, the cheese is piled with sun-dried tomatoes tossed with honey, balsamic, and herbs before it's baked. Serve the melty wheel in the center of a platter, surrounded by the slaw, and let everyone scoop up generous portions of both.

While a standard wheel of Brie will do just fine, I do think this salad deserves special treatment, given that it's a bit indulgent. Harbison is a bloomy-rind cheese from Jasper Hill Farm in Vermont that I am mildly obsessed with. It's shamelessly creamy, a bit stinky (in a good way), and both sweet and vegetal, making it much more complex than your average grocery store wheel. Look for it at your local specialty cheese shop or Whole Foods, or check out the Jasper Hill website and treat yourself to a mixed box of cheeses.

ARRANGE A RACK in the middle of the oven and heat the oven to 300°F. Line a small rimmed baking sheet with parchment paper.

Quarter the cabbage through its core and season the cabbage wedges all over with salt and pepper. Heat 1 tablespoon of the olive oil in a large cast-iron or other heavy-bottomed skillet over medium-high heat until shimmering. Place 2 cabbage wedges with a cut side down in the pan and cook, undisturbed, until well charred on the bottom, about 3 minutes. Carefully flip and continue to cook until the other cut side is well-charred, about

3 minutes more. Transfer to a cutting board to cool slightly and repeat with 1 tablespoon olive oil and the remaining 2 wedges.

Meanwhile, combine the sun-dried tomatoes, honey, oregano, 1 teaspoon vinegar, and red pepper flakes in a small bowl. Whisk together the remaining 2 tablespoons vinegar, remaining 1 tablespoon olive oil, a generous pinch of salt, and several grinds of black pepper in a large bowl.

Core the cabbage wedges, then thinly slice the wedges crosswise and add to the bowl of dressing along with the parsley and scallions. Toss to coat in the vinaigrette. Taste and season with additional salt and black pepper as needed. Set aside.

If using a wheel of Harbison cheese, remove the spruce bark wrap from around the wheel. Place the cheese on the prepared baking sheet and spoon the sun-dried tomato mixture on top (it's okay if some of it falls over the edges). Bake until the cheese wheel is still intact, but the cheese is soft and melty, 5 to 10 minutes. (Keep a close eye on it, as it can go from soft to totally collapsed quite quickly.)

Carefully transfer the baked cheese wheel and any sun-dried tomatoes that have fallen onto the baking sheet to the center of a serving platter with a wide spatula. Don't worry too much if it collapses a bit in the process—this is an intentionally rustic-looking salad and a little messy is okay! Pile the slaw around the cheese on the platter and drizzle the cheese and slaw with a bit more honey. Serve with a big spoon to scoop up portions of the melty cheese with slaw.

Bagna Cauda Salad
with Frico Fried Eggs

SERVES 4

½ cup water

6 cloves garlic, gently
smashed and peeled

12 oil-packed anchovy
fillets, drained

⅓ cup plus 1 tablespoon
extra-virgin olive oil,
divided

2 ounces Parmesan
cheese, freshly grated
(1 packed cup)

4 large eggs

Kosher salt

5 ounces torn frisée
or curly endive (about
5 packed cups)

1 medium Belgian endive,
halved and sliced into
roughly ½-inch ribbons

1 small or ½ medium
fennel bulb, trimmed,
quartered, and very thinly
sliced with a mandoline
or knife

1 (12-ounce) jar roasted
red peppers, drained,
patted dry, and torn into
bite-sized pieces

Freshly ground black
pepper

½ small lemon,
for serving

If you're unfamiliar with bagna cauda, allow me to introduce you. The warm garlic and anchovy dip from the northwestern Piedmont region of Italy translates to "hot bath" and is precisely that. It's a simple yet shamelessly pungent mix of melted anchovies, garlic, and olive oil that's served with raw and cooked vegetables for dipping.

I've been enchanted by bagna cauda ever since living in its birthplace and learning how to make it from a local classmate. Hopefully, she won't mind this unconventional interpretation, where the dip is turned into a dressing for a mix of vegetables that often go for a swim in it. For completeness, an egg fried in frico—melted-until-golden, cracker-like Parmesan cheese—is slid on top of each bowl. This is a brazen salad that's worth the effort.

PLACE THE WATER and garlic cloves in a small saucepan and bring to a simmer over medium heat. Reduce the heat to low and simmer very gently, stirring occasionally, until the garlic is softened and easily squished with the back of a spoon, about 10 minutes.

Drain the garlic, wipe the saucepan dry, and return the garlic to it. Add the anchovies and ⅓ cup olive oil and cook over low heat, smashing the anchovies and garlic and stirring frequently, until the mixture is very fragrant, the anchovies are almost completely dissolved, and the garlic is falling apart but not browned, 10 to 15 minutes.

Remove the pot from the heat and, if needed, smash and stir the anchovies and garlic a bit more until the mixture is mostly (though likely not completely) smooth. Let cool slightly while you fry the eggs.

Heat 1 tablespoon olive oil in a large nonstick skillet over medium heat until shimmering. Sprinkle the Parmesan in an even layer to cover the bottom of the pan. Cook until the cheese begins to melt, about 30 seconds.

recipe continues . . .

Crack the eggs onto the cheese, season with a pinch of salt, then cover the pan and cook until the eggs are just barely set but not yet cooked through, 1 to 2 minutes. Uncover and continue to cook until the cheese is crisp and golden brown, and the egg whites are set and the yolks are runny, 2 to 3 minutes more. Use a spatula to help lift and slide the frico fried eggs onto a cutting board.

Place the frisée, endive, fennel, and roasted red peppers in a large bowl. Drizzle the bagna cauda over the vegetables and toss to coat. Divide the salad among 4 shallow bowls. Cut the frico fried eggs into individual fried eggs and divide among the salads. If there are any crispy cheese shards that break off after cutting, sprinkle them over the salads along with several grinds of pepper and a squeeze of lemon juice.

Brûléed Citrus Salad

SERVES 4

¼ cup raw hazelnuts

¼ cup packed light or
dark brown sugar

½ teaspoon orange
blossom water, rose
water, or vanilla extract

Kosher salt

2 medium blood, Cara
Cara, or navel oranges,
or a combination

1 medium grapefruit,
any variety

Finely grated zest of
½ medium lime

Freshly squeezed juice
of ½ medium lime
(about 1 tablespoon)

¼ cup lemon curd

Citrus is a lifeline during the doldrums of winter, and this salad is a sunny pleasure. Orange blossom water or rose water adds a uniquely floral note that won't overpower the fruit, so long as you stick to the tiniest splash, while toasted hazelnuts provide sweet crunch, and lemon curd bolsters the salad's wonderful tartness and offsets each juicy forkful with a bit of creamy richness.

ARRANGE ONE RACK in the middle of the oven and another rack in the top third of the oven (6 to 8 inches from the broiling element) and heat the oven to 350°F.

Spread the hazelnuts out on a small rimmed baking sheet and toast in the oven, stirring halfway through, until fragrant and golden brown, 8 to 10 minutes.

Meanwhile, combine the brown sugar, flower water or vanilla extract, and a pinch of salt in a large bowl.

Trim the tops and bottoms from the oranges and grapefruit so that they rest flat on the cutting board. Cut away the peel and pith, following the curve of the fruit, then cut the fruit crosswise into ½-inch-thick rounds and remove any seeds.

Once the nuts are toasted, remove from the oven and switch the oven to broil on high.

Add the citrus to the bowl with brown sugar. Toss the fruit with your hands, then transfer to a rimmed baking sheet in a single layer, leaving the sugary juices in the bowl; reserve.

Broil the citrus on the top rack, rotating the pan halfway through, until the fruit is caramelized, about 10 minutes. Transfer the pan to a wire rack to cool for 5 minutes.

Meanwhile, wrap the toasted hazelnuts in a clean kitchen towel and rub vigorously to remove as much of the skins as possible (don't worry about any skin that doesn't easily come off). Transfer the nuts to a cutting board and coarsely chop.

Whisk 1 tablespoon juice from the bowl, the lime zest, and lime juice together in a small bowl.

Transfer the brûléed citrus to a serving platter. Drizzle with the dressing, dollop with lemon curd, and sprinkle with hazelnuts.

Earl Grey–Poached Dates over Caramel Crème Fraîche

SERVES 4

———

½ cup granulated sugar

1¼ cups water, divided

½ teaspoon flaky sea salt, plus more for serving

½ cup crème fraîche, at room temperature

2 tablespoons cold unsalted butter, cut into cubes

1 teaspoon vanilla extract

2 Earl Grey tea bags, or 2 teaspoons loose Earl Grey tea

12 Medjool dates, halved lengthwise and pitted

½ cup heavy cream

6 gingersnap cookies (about 1½ ounces), crushed

Dates are so deeply sweet and candy-like, they're practically dessert all on their own. My husband, however, would never buy into this truth. So, I duped him by bringing caramel cream and cookies to the party—the latter almost always does the trick. This is a luxurious way to end a meal on a cold winter night. But don't be too fooled: The soft, chewy dates are the star here, though piling them onto a little creamy decadence absolutely doesn't hurt.

PLACE THE SUGAR, ¼ cup of the water, and flaky sea salt in a medium saucepan. Set the mixture over medium heat and swirl occasionally until the sugar dissolves and the mixture is clear, glossy, and just beginning to bubble, about 2 minutes. Increase the heat to medium-high and cook, undisturbed, until the sugar begins to turn golden brown, 2 to 3 minutes. Swirl gently a few times to ensure the sugar is cooking evenly and continue to cook until the sugar is dark amber, about 1 minute more. Immediately remove the pan from the heat and very carefully (the mixture will bubble up aggressively) whisk in the crème fraîche until smooth. Add the butter and vanilla and whisk until the butter has melted and the caramel is smooth. Pour into a medium heatproof bowl and transfer to the refrigerator, stirring occasionally to hasten cooling, and chill until at least room temperature, about 30 minutes.

Meanwhile, bring the remaining 1 cup water to a boil in a small saucepan over high heat. Remove from the heat, add the tea, and steep for 5 minutes. Discard the tea bags or, if using loose tea, strain the tea leaves through a fine-mesh strainer, discard the leaves, and return the tea to the saucepan.

Bring the tea to a boil over high heat, add the dates, reduce the heat to medium-low, and simmer, stirring occasionally, until the dates have plumped and the liquid has reduced by over half, 8 to 10 minutes. Remove from the heat and set aside.

Once the caramel is at least room temperature and no longer warm, pour the heavy cream into the bowl of a stand mixer

fitted with the whisk attachment or a large bowl, if using a hand mixer. Beat on medium-high speed until soft peaks form, 3 to 5 minutes. Gently fold in the caramel until just combined.

Divide the caramel whipped cream mixture among 4 shallow dessert bowls or plates. Use a slotted spoon to divide the poached dates among the bowls. If there is any poaching liquid left in the saucepan, drizzle a bit over the dates. Sprinkle with crushed gingersnaps and garnish with a pinch of flaky sea salt.

Shaved Pears and Chocolate with Amaretti Crumble

SERVES 4

2 ounces small crunchy amaretti cookies (about eighteen 1¼-inch cookies)

3 tablespoons raw whole almonds

2 tablespoons all-purpose flour

1 tablespoon light or dark brown sugar

¼ teaspoon ground cinnamon

¼ teaspoon kosher salt

2 tablespoons cold unsalted butter, cut into cubes

2 firm but ripe medium pears, such as D'Anjou or Bosc (about 1 pound)

Juice of ½ medium lemon (about 1½ tablespoons)

1 ounce bittersweet or dark chocolate (60% to 70% cacao)

Extra-virgin olive oil, for serving

Flaky sea salt, for serving

Crunchy Italian amaretti cookies, also called amaretti di Saronno, are a fun ingredient to play around with. While you can of course pair a couple with your espresso, they're so packed with bittersweet almond flavor, that's really just the beginning. You can grind them into a flour-like consistency to use in cakes, turn them into a crust for tarts or cheesecakes à la graham crackers, or add them to a fruit crumble topping. Using them as a crumble is the approach here, except you'll bake it separately to create sweet and crunchy contrast for a bowl of juicy shaved pears and dark chocolate. It's an understated dessert that feels special.

ARRANGE A RACK in the middle of the oven and heat the oven to 375°F. Line a rimmed baking sheet with parchment paper.

Place the amaretti cookies in the bowl of a food processor fitted with the blade attachment. Pulse until coarsely ground, about 10 pulses. Add the almonds, flour, brown sugar, cinnamon, and kosher salt and pulse until the almonds just start to break up, about 8 pulses. Add the butter and pulse until large, heavy crumbs form and no dry spots remain, about 30 pulses.

Transfer the crumble mixture to the prepared baking sheet in a single layer, squeezing it into large clumps with your hands in the process. Bake, gently tossing halfway through, until golden brown and firm to the touch, 8 to 10 minutes.

Meanwhile, quarter, core, and very thinly slice the pears (there is no need to peel them unless you prefer to). Place in a large bowl, drizzle with lemon juice, and toss to coat. Transfer the pears to a serving bowl or platter.

Once the crumble is ready, let it cool for 10 minutes, then sprinkle it over the pears. Shave the chocolate with a vegetable peeler or paring knife over the top, then drizzle with a bit of olive oil and sprinkle with a few pinches of flaky sea salt.

Acknowledgments

NOTHING BRINGS ME more joy than creating and sharing recipes and then seeing them come to life in home kitchens. Thank you to those who have supported my big ambitions and rooted for me along the way.

Thank you . . .
To Max Sinsheimer, my literary agent, for your constant enthusiasm and belief in me, along with your tireless support.

To Rizzoli, especially my editor, Tricia Levi, associate publisher, Jim Muschett, and designer, Jan Derevjanik, for your rooted faith in me and my vision.

To Kristin Teig and Catrine Kelty, my dream photo team, for your incredible talent and for continuing on this cookbook journey with me.

To my family, especially Dad and Tara, along with my wonderful friends, colleagues, and mentors for being my cheerleaders and eager recipe testers. And to Mom, in my heart and head and guiding me always.

And of course, to my love Joe, for eating salad after salad when you'd probably have preferred to order a pizza.

Index

About the Author

SHEELA PRAKASH IS a food and wine writer, recipe developer, and the author of *Mediterranean Every Day: Simple, Inspired Recipes for Feel-Good Food*. She is a longtime editor at Kitchn, and has been on staff at Epicurious and Food52. Her writing and recipes can be found in such online and print publications as *Better Homes & Gardens*, *Real Simple*, Simply Recipes, Serious Eats, Tasting Table, The Splendid Table, and *Culture Cheese Magazine*. Sheela received a master's degree in Food Culture & Communications at the Slow Food–founded University of Gastronomic Sciences in Italy, holds Level 2 and Level 3 Awards in Wines from the Wine & Spirit Education Trust, and is also a registered dietitian.

First published in the United States
of America in 2023
by Rizzoli International
Publications, Inc.
300 Park Avenue South
New York, NY 10010
www.rizzoliusa.com

Copyright © 2023
Sheela Prakash

Photographer: Kristin Teig
Photo Stylist: Catrine Kelty

Publisher: Charles Miers
Associate Publisher:
James Muschett
Editor: Tricia Levi
Designer: Jan Derevjanik
Production Manager:
Colin Hough Trapp
Managing Editor: Lynn Scrabis

Printed in China

2024 2025 2026 2027 /
10 9 8 7 6 5 4 3

ISBN: 978-0-8478-9926-5
Library of Congress Control
Number: 2022945513

Visit us online:
Facebook.com/RizzoliNewYork
Twitter: @Rizzoli_Books
Instagram.com/RizzoliBooks
Pinterest.com/RizzoliBooks
Youtube.com/user/RizzoliNY
Issuu.com/Rizzoli